This cheerful, lively, and [...] adults alike to a better [...] live in and a greater aw[...] [...] it all. In a discussion often dominated by prejudice and fear, this book will enable Christians from all backgrounds to engage with the real questions and to find their faith strengthened.

> **Tom Wright,** *Former Bishop of Durham, now Professor of New Testament and Early Christianity, University of St Andrews*

This is a really cool, funny, entertaining book in which you'll learn a lot about science as well as faith along the way. And my guess is that your parents will read it as well!

> **Denis Alexander,** *Emeritus Director of The Faraday Institute for Science and Religion, St. Edmund's College, University of Cambridge*

This book is really excellent – properly funny and not cringey as these things can so easily be, and a really heartening and encouraging read for Christian children with enquiring minds. I can't wait to buy a copy for my ten-year-old son!

> **Sophie Hutton-Squire,** *Mother*

This amazing story will have every reader gripped. Sam Billington pursues a quest with his school chums to discover how to relate his curiosity about how the world works to what different grown-ups tell him he ought to believe. An absolute page-turner by a celebrated children's writer and one of Europe's top scientists.

> **Andrew Briggs,** *Professor of Nanomaterials, University of Oxford*

A great, funny, and warm book that encourages questioning and conversation about faith and science. Brilliant for grown ups and kids to read and enjoy together. Inspiration for future generations of faith-filled scientists!

Kate Bottley, BBC pastor and part of the Gogglebox family on Channel 4

The cosmos and the living world impress all of us, whether religious or not (and I am not) with a sense of mystery and wonder. Readers will learn a lot from this engaging and fascinating book. As we learn more about nature, some mysteries are dispelled – but the wonder grows.

Martin Rees, Former President of the Royal Society, Astronomer Royal, Professor of Cosmology and Astrophysics, University of Cambridge

In this delightful book, full of adventure and humour, ten-year-old Sam Billington, a budding young scientist, learns about the Big Bang and evolution and discovers what this means for Christian faith. With a positive message about science and faith, this book is highly recommended for children and even adults.

Ard Louis, Professor in Physics, Oxford University

A delightfully written book with a serious purpose – how to bridge the apparent chasm between science and faith. *Science Geek Sam* ably shows there is no chasm at all, and does so triumphantly. Full of fun facts, up-to-date on the science, and with a mature take on Biblical truth, this is a book every child should read with an open mind, and one which parents can trust too. At last children can see that both science and Christianity can be respected at the same time.

Dominic Couzens, Birder, speaker, tour leader, natural history writer for BBC Wildlife and Bird Watching

In a fast-moving and utterly delightful way these colourful Year 6 pupils puzzle their way through the big questions of the universe. They puzzle and wonder at stars, planets, the age of the earth, and the evolution of life (and who likes whom at school of course). The book's breathtaking speed nonetheless gives them (and the reader) a serious and thought-provoking treatment. The question of God runs through the book in an unaffected way as they work through to a natural holding of science and Christian belief together. I would happily give this charming book to any thoughtful youngster.

Tom McLeish, *Professor of Physics, Durham University*

If every young person, parent, and teacher read this book, the world would be a gentler place. Not everybody would agree with each other about the Big Bang and evolution, but all would see that embracing science is part of the Christian experience. Many of us can relate to Sam Billington, who thinks fossils and stars and DNA are totally awesome, but who has honest questions about God and the Bible. Not everyone is lucky enough to have an Uncle Jack, a busy science professor who regularly, gently, and truthfully engages Sam's questions. What makes the book fun but also believable are the relationships between Sam, his classmates, and their teacher Mr Nolan, who creates space to ask and investigate hard questions. And far from being a dry book of science facts, there are enough kid-friendly jokes to keep readers laughing.

Deborah Haarsma, *Professor of Astronomy and President of BioLogos*

Science GEEK SAM

and his secret LOGBOOK

Corien Oranje and Cees Dekker

Translated by Petra Crofton-van Rijssen
and Sophie van Houtryve

LION
CHILDREN'S

Published by Lion Children's Books
an imprint of
Lion Hudson IP Ltd
Wilkinson House, Jordan Hill Road,
Oxford OX2 8DR, England
www.lionhudson.com/lionchildrens

ISBN 978 0 7459 7724 9

Originally published in Dutch under the title: *Het geheime
logboek van topnerd Tycho* by Corien Oranje and Cees Dekker
Copyright © 2015 Uitgeverij Columbus, Heerenveen,
The Netherlands
Uitgeverij Columbus is part of Royal Jongbloed Publishers

Acknowledgments
Front cover and prelim illustrations: Sam © Doodlemachine/
istock; book © Vladgrin/istock; rocket, planet, telescope, flask
© suirey/istock; dinosaur © Robert Adrian Hillman/Shutterstock
Back cover illustrations: doodles © Sophie Foster

A catalogue record for this book is available from the British
Library

Printed and bound in the UK, September 2017, LH26

This is the TOP SECRET logbook of Sam Billington
with my discoveries, and questions about everything I've yet to solve.

ACCESS STRICTLY FORBIDDEN!!

If you find this book, email me!
sambillington06@hotmail.com

LOG ⭐

My name:	Sam Billington
Favourite food:	sausages and chips
Favourite number:	3.14159265358979323846264338327950288419716939937510582097494459230781640628 6
Favourite hobby:	digging up old things (like fossils and dinosaur bones)
Best friend:	Archie
Sister:	Lottie
Brother:	Snotty Simon
My dad:	Norman Billington (cheese-shop owner)
My mum:	Lydia Billington (cheese-shop owner)
Favourite teacher:	Mr Nolan!!!
Person I'd swap with for a day:	Tim Peake (astronaut)
If I could travel in time:	I'd go back to AD 33 to Israel, to shadow Jesus and see what he gets up to (I especially want to see him walk on water and watch his friends' jaws drop when they think they're seeing a ghost!)

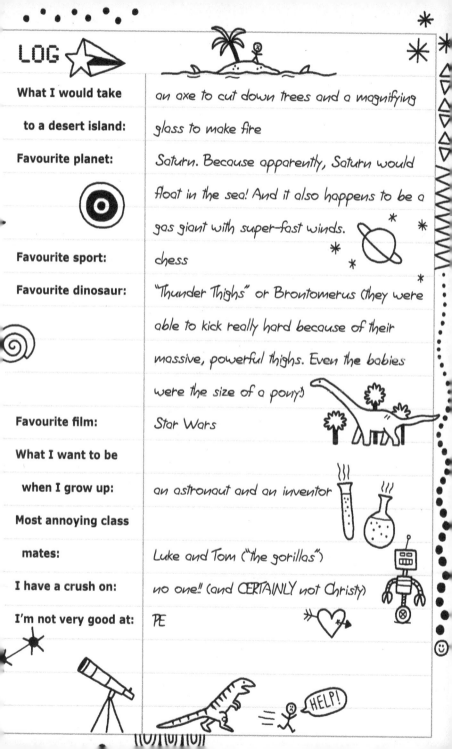

LOG

What I would take to a desert island:	an axe to cut down trees and a magnifying glass to make fire
Favourite planet:	Saturn. Because apparently, Saturn would float in the sea! And it also happens to be a gas giant with super-fast winds.
Favourite sport:	chess
Favourite dinosaur:	"Thunder Thighs" or Brontomerus (they were able to kick really hard because of their massive, powerful thighs. Even the babies were the size of a pony!)
Favourite film:	Star Wars
What I want to be when I grow up:	an astronaut and an inventor
Most annoying class mates:	Luke and Tom ("the gorillas")
I have a crush on:	no one!! (and CERTAINLY not Christy)
I'm not very good at:	PE

HELP!

TUESDAY MORNING

First I heard a whistling sound – like in a cartoon, when Bugs Bunny drops out of the sky. And then, a bang. Not just thunder or fireworks exploding; no, this was a

SUPERMEGAULTRA LOUDBANGBANG BOOMTHIS-IS-THE-END-OF-THE-WORLD

kind of bang!!

Which became even louder because all of a sudden the windows shattered, and broken glass was scattered all over the floor. And because some of the kids started screaming. And because Matteo, who never sits still, fell off his chair onto the floor and accidentally pulled the table down, too.

"A bomb," Luke cried.

"Woohoo!" screamed Tom. "Gunpowder! They're lighting gunpowder."

"Fire!" Florence called. That was pure nonsense of course because there was no fire whatsoever, just smoke and dust and shards of glass that made a crunchy noise when we walked on them. Loads of people were screaming their heads off, and Anna

shouted: "I'm bleeding! Mr Nolan! There's blood on my hand! And I've got glass in my hair!"

Matteo had jumped up again. "Look!" he called out. "Look at the bike shed." I ran over to the window to have a look. Wooaaah. The bike and scooter shed had collapsed entirely and was lying in a mangled mess.

"Told you!" said Luke. "It's a bomb. Someone has attacked our school!"

"Or maybe someone crashed into the scooter shed!" Archie suggested. "Perhaps a parachutist, with a parachute that never opened."

"Let me check it out," I said. "In case they need help."

I ran to the door. As long as I don't need to give the kiss of life, I thought. That is just so gross. Right then, the fire alarm went off. TINGTINGTINGTING. The noise was ear-splitting.

"Mr Nolan!" Archie called. "Fire drill."

"Duhhh!" replied Christy. "This isn't a drill, this is for real."

"Form a line in pairs," Mr Nolan called. "Stay calm. All of you, stay calm! *Where* is the register? Where?!"

"It's over there, on the hook on the door, Sir," I said. And off we went. Out of the classroom, along the corridor. The fire alarm just went on and on and on.

We could see the Year One children leaving their classroom and walking down the stairs in pairs, holding hands and singing: "We'll go down together all in a row. We're not in a hurry, we'll be quiet as we go!" The Reception class children were carrying chairs. I guess their brand-new classroom assistant didn't know you should leave everything behind when the fire alarm goes off. Probably keen to save the chairs. The Year Five pupils emerged from their classrooms, and so did the Year Threes and Fours. The corridors were crowded, children pushing and shoving to the left and to the right. Miss Smith from Year Two was standing in the hall, trying to control the flow of children.

"Everyone go to the playground!" she shouted. However, it was very hard to know which playground she meant because she squints.

"No! Not the BIG playground! Go to the INFANTS' playground!"

"We're not in a hurry," the Year Ones sang...

TINGTINGTINGTINGTINGTING. The fire alarm kept going. TINGTINGTINGTING.

"Can someone please switch it off!" Archie cried. "It's driving me insane."

Someone pushed me, so I bashed into Tom.

"Oi!" he reacted angrily. "Watch where you're going, geek!"

"I couldn't help it," I said. "I was pushed." I tripped over a toddler chair in the corridor and fell flat on my face. Tom and Luke laughed loudly and a few of the infants scrambled over my legs.

"SAM BILLINGTON!" Miss Smith bellowed. "GET UP IMMEDIATELY!"

"Come on!" Archie pulled me up and together we made it to the exit. All of the children were outside by now. Luke and Tom were trying to get onto the roof by climbing a drainpipe, a few of the Reception children were fighting over the ride-on toys, and a little boy was standing in the middle of the sandpit throwing handfuls of sand in the air. All the teachers were talking to each other, while trying to calm the children down.

TINGTINGTINGTINGTINGTINGTING

"Shall I phone 999?" Archie asked.

"Let's find out what's going on first," I said. I looked at the teachers, but they were far too busy on their phones to keep an eye on us.

"Come on," I said, and we ran behind the school and climbed over the fence that separates the infants' and the juniors' playgrounds.

What we saw there was just incredible. What a mess! The playground was littered with bent pieces of corrugated iron, lumps of rock, and shards of glass. And where ten minutes ago the bike shed had been, there was now just a pile of twisted and overturned scooters and bikes. And there was a hole in the ground. An enormous hole, at least a metre deep. A few elderly people were staring at the scene from a safe distance and more spectators were coming towards the school. There were ladies with bags of groceries, a man in a wheelchair, a few tall lads holding sausage rolls, and a mum with a trailer bike.

"What's wrong with kids these days!" an elderly man said.

"I bet they were playing with fireworks," the man in the wheelchair chipped in.

"I can't believe they get away with it. And this is meant to be a Christian school."

"Well, there you go."

"They're a bunch of hooligans."

"Look at that hole in the ground!"

"Those were no ordinary fireworks."

TINGTINGTINGTINGTINGTINGTING

The fire alarm just didn't stop. It made a shrill noise that went right through you. I ran towards the shed to see more of what was going on. I stepped across some broken bikes and looked at the hole in the ground. I couldn't see any arms or legs, so it hadn't been a parachutist crashing into the shed. What a relief – at least I didn't have to give anyone the kiss of life. But what on earth had happened? A bomb? Who would drop a bomb onto the bike shed of Trinity Primary School?

"Maybe it was a toilet," Archie said. "A toilet that fell out of a plane. I read in the paper once that a Boeing lost its toilet. If a toilet falls down from 10,000 metres high, it will make a massive hole in the ground."

"That wasn't a loo, man," I said. "That was poo. Frozen poo that fell out of the plane."

We carefully peered into the hole. No toilet. And nothing that resembled poo. All I saw was soil and stones. But perhaps frozen poo looks like stone?

Suddenly we heard loud sirens coming our way, closer and closer, until the noise was deafening. It was so overwhelming that you couldn't hear the TINGTINGTING of the fire alarm anymore. A large, red fire engine pulled up and turned around on the playground, followed by two police cars. They switched off the sirens and five firemen came running down the playground, while two policemen marking the area with red and white tape.

"Move back, move back!" they called out. "Everyone move out of the way, please."

A few ordinary cars drove onto the playground and men in white outfits jumped out. I felt like we were in a movie.

"This is epic," I said to Archie.

"More epic than geography," Archie said.

There was Christy. "Sam! Everybody's looking for you!"

"We're just checking out what's going on," I said.

"Sir, Sir! We found them!" she called to Mr Nolan.

"There you are," Mr Nolan said, as he came running up, flustered and out of breath. "I was getting worried about you boys."

Whoops. Yes. We suddenly remembered that we were supposed to stay together as a group if the fire alarm went off, until we were allowed back in the classroom. On the other hand, there was no fire and it was just the shed that had collapsed.

"We just wanted to know what'd happened," I said. I expected Mr Nolan to get really cross, but he just summoned us to go back to the infants' playground, where Mr Fazeli, the head was standing on the edge of the sandpit next to a police officer.

"Well, we all had a terrible fright, of course," he began. "But thankfully, no one got hurt."

"I'm bleeding!" Anna shouted, and she showed off her hand so all of us could see.

"... I mean, no one was seriously injured," Mr Fazeli continued.

"What about me? I could have lost my arm!" Anna exclaimed. "And I had glass in my hair!"

"Excuse me, officer," Matteo called. "Was it a bomb from a plane?"

"At the moment we don't know what has happened," the policeman said. "We're in the middle of finding out. But one thing is for certain: you're not allowed to go back into the school."

"Yippeeee!" cried Tom, and Luke did his crazy dance move. Everyone was cheering and clapping.

"A day off!"

"Whoopee!"

"Let's go and play football!"

"Let's go to the sweet shop!"

Mr Fazeli raised his hand. This means we have to be quiet. Every teacher raised their hand, as did the children, until everyone had gone quiet – except for Tom and Luke, who were busy talking about the sweets they wanted to buy.

"Gobstoppers!"

"No, chocolate!"

"Gobstoppers are the best!" Christy dug Tom in the ribs and it was only when Tom went to punch her back that he realized everyone had raised their hand. He quickly put up his fist, and so did Luke. At last everyone was quiet.

"We're contacting all your parents and carers," Mr Fazeli said. "As soon as they've arrived to collect you, you can go."

"But I always go home by myself!" Archie said.

"Me too!"

"My mum won't come over to get me. Seriously."

"I can go home on my own on my bike, no problem."

"I'm afraid you won't be able to cycle home today, boys," Mr Fazeli replied. "Your bikes are broken and until we know what has happened, you're not allowed anywhere near the big playground."

"But my bike was brand new!"

"Can I please go and have a look to see if my scooter is still there, Sir?"

"I live opposite the school, Sir, can I please just go home?"

Mr Fazeli could NOT be persuaded. We all had to be collected by a parent or carer, or an after-school club leader. One after another, the children were collected and soon the playground was empty. Even Archie had gone home and my sister Lottie had gone with a friend. It was just Luke, Tom, and me who were still waiting. How long would I be stuck here? Maybe until eight o'clock this evening? My parents wouldn't come. They're not nasty or anything but they're just too busy to check their phones. We get tons of Japanese tourists wanting to take selfies with my parents in front of their cheeses and the old-fashioned scales.

"Would Sam be able to go home with you, please?" Mr Nolan asked Tom's mum.

"Yes, of course," she said. "I'm taking Luke home, too."

"What?" Tom asked. "No way are we taking Sam!"

"What do you mean?" replied his mum. "Don't be rude! Of course we'll take him."

"No, no. It won't be necessary," I quickly chipped in. I really didn't fancy going to Tom's house, especially not with Luke in tow as well. Last time I went to Tom's, he made us play hide-and-seek then him and Luke locked me in the garage. They left me there for TWO hours.

"Hey, Sam!" a voice called out. I turned around and saw my Uncle Jack.

"Hi, Uncle Jack, what are you doing here?"

"Good!" Mr Nolan said, sounding relieved. "That's all sorted then. OK, boys. I'm going back inside for a staff meeting. I'll text or phone your parents tonight with an update."

TUESDAY AFTERNOON

Honest. I wouldn't want to swap my mum and dad for anyone or anything (not even for a thousand quid – although that could buy me an awesome new laptop), but my Uncle Jack, he's something else – he's VERY cool. Uncle Jack is my mum's youngest brother and he knows EVERYTHING about stars and planets. I've been to his house a few times to look at the stars at night. He has a REAL telescope. I bet it would even allow you to see a rocket land on the moon.

"Did Mum send you to collect me?" I asked.

"Collect you?" Uncle Jack was surprised. "No, I'm here to investigate the crash in the playground."

"You mean the loud bang?" I replied.

"Yes, that's it," Uncle Jack nodded. "We want to see if it was caused by a meteorite."

"A meteorite?" I shouted. "From space? Really? That is so cool!"

"We don't know yet what caused it. It would be tremendous if it was a meteorite. These things only happen once in a hundred years."

Wow. That would be so awesome, if our bike shed had been hit by a meteorite.

"Can I help?" I offered. "School's finished early."

"I think you'd better go home, Sam," said Uncle Jack.

"I can't. There's no one at home."

"I'll give your mum a ring now." Uncle Jack got his phone out and marched off to the big playground. I ran after him, past the sand pit and climbing frame.

"Mr Nolan has already tried," I protested. "They didn't answer and they never pick up texts, either. They're far too busy." Uncle Jack stepped over the fence. I followed him. There weren't just firefighters and men in white outfits and police officers on the playground anymore. Now I could also see photographers, cameramen, and journalists scribbling busily in their notepads. The area where the scooter and bike shed had been was cordoned off.

I tapped Uncle Jack on his back. "If I did go home, there won't be anyone there."

Uncle Jack turned around. "No one?"

"No, on a Tuesday I always go to our neighbour, Sue, but she only gets home at three, so I'd be waiting on her doorstep for four hours. Stuck outside."

Uncle Jack stepped over the red and white tape and peered at the hole in the ground. This was the hole where there'd been a shed until this morning.

"I was here when it happened," I said. "I can tell you everything. The funny whistling sound, the explosion, the enormous bang. Imagine if I'd been in the shed just when it happened? I would have been flat as a pancake. Or a shard of glass could have sliced me in half." I tried to shiver, so Uncle Jack would think I was all upset. "I'm no wimp but I was really shaken up by that."

"Hey, you there!" A man with a beard called in our direction. "Come over here and help me out with this, will you?" I looked around but he was talking to me. "We're trying to tidy this place up and you look like you need something to do."

I helped move bikes and scooters (my bike had two crooked wheels, some of the spokes had disappeared, and the front tyre was punctured). I swept the playground and carried bits of corrugated iron and fragmented wood to the chestnut tree. Uncle Jack and a few other men were lying on their fronts around the hole. They were gently sweeping small brushes across the soil, as if they were looking for diamonds. Or bombs, of course.

At last, Uncle Jack put his hand all the way down into the hole. With a white glove he lifted out a stone which looked a bit like a badly burnt doughnut. He carefully placed it in a box filled with cotton wool and closed the lid.

"Is it a meteorite?" I asked.

Uncle Jack got up and took off his gloves. He was beaming. "It looks like it," he said. "I can't wait to take a closer look and find out for sure."

"You can't be serious," Mum said, perplexed. "What if it had hit the school?!"

"It was only a small one," Uncle Jack responded. "I wonder if it would have gone through the roof of the school."

"Well..." I started. "It did go right through the—"

Uncle Jack interrupted. "This is a remarkable event, Lydia! A beautiful meteorite. Most meteorites land in the ocean, or in other uninhabited places. This is so rare. We are extremely fortunate."

"Fortunate?" Mum exclaimed. "Do you call that fortunate?"

"Not fortunate that it landed on the shed," Uncle Jack quickly added. "But that we managed to find it. That we can study it."

Mum rolled her eyes. "I can't believe this is my brother speaking. My eldest son has just escaped death – it was touch-and-go – and all you can say is how happy you are that you found a meteorite."

"If it's a real one; we don't know yet."

"Pfff," scoffed Mum.

Now it was Uncle Jack who rolled his eyes. He collapsed onto the sofa, put his feet up on the coffee table, and looked at the ceiling. "You know what? I hope we'll find some amino acids. Or lipids."

"What are amino acids?" I asked.

"Amino acids are in cheese," Mum snapped. "They're just protein. I don't think you'll find protein in a meteorite, Jack."

"Amino acids are not protein," Uncle Jack replied. "They are the building blocks that make protein. The building blocks for life. And if we find amino acids on a meteorite from outer space, well..."

"... Then a piece of cheese must have crumbled off the moon,"

Mum snapped back. She picked Simon up, who had been playing at her feet, wiped his snotty nose, and walked off to the kitchen.

"She doesn't really like science," I said.

Uncle Jack left. We ate sausages and mashed potatoes with bits of kale and I created a volcano with gravy in the crater (the gravy was the lava).

"I hope they can go back to school as usual tomorrow," Dad said.

"Absolutely," said Mum. She popped a spoonful of kale and potato in Simon's mouth. Simon pushed the food back out with his tongue, and the green mash, mixed with saliva, dripped down his chin. "I hope so, too. Otherwise the kids will just have to come along to the shop."

Shocked, I dropped my sausage in the crater and the gravy splattered all around. "Please, nooo!"

"Hmm, that would actually be quite useful," Dad said. "They can help me fill up the nut and cheese trays."

"Nooo!" I groaned.

"Yeah, cool!" Lottie said. She's always extremely annoying, such a goody-goody.

"I'd like to get them some aprons to wear in the shop," said Mum. "The customers will think it's cute."

"Yesss!" shouted Lottie.

"NOOOO!" I exclaimed. At that moment, the phone rang. It was Archie.

"Sam!" he cried excitedly.

"Why are you shouting?" I asked.

"We're on TV!"

"Oh yeah, sure," I said. "Very funny."

"Haven't you seen it? We're on Newsround!"

"What?!" I ran to the lounge, grabbed the remote control and switched the TV on.

"A woman spray paints dog poo pink," CBBC's Katie announced. "Prince George receives 700 presents for his birthday. And the children of Trinity Primary School escape disaster by the skin of their teeth."

Dad dropped his fork, Mum pulled Simon out of his chair, Lottie jumped up, and all five of us sat around the TV. First they showed this lady walking around a large meadow, spray painting every piece of dog poo she could find a shade of dirty pink. Next up was Prince George, being showered with birthday presents. At last, our school was on.

"The pupils of Trinity Primary School were given a terrible fright this morning when their bike shed was smashed to pieces after being hit by an unknown object." The camera moved slowly around the playground and stopped where the shed had been.

"This is Mr Silan Fazeli, head of Trinity Primary School. Mr Fazeli, tell us, what happened?"

"It was just before our lunch break," said Mr Fazeli. "We heard a whistling sound followed by an enormous bang. When I looked outside, the bike shed had gone."

"What did you think had happened?"

"Firecrackers, I thought. Or perhaps a firework bomb," said Mr Fazeli. "I immediately pressed the fire alarm and we evacuated all the pupils."

The camera turned to the reporter. "A bomb made of fireworks – that is what the school head thought. But researchers discovered that the shed was hit by a rock. No ordinary one, but a meteorite, a lump of waste from outer space that is billions of years old."

"Really?" said Mum. "Who would believe that? Billions of years? Rubbish."

"Thankfully no one was hurt," the reporter continued, "but the children did all have to walk home today, as their bikes and scooters were written off. And because of the powerful shock all the windows smashed. As you can see, workmen are making a real effort to replace the glass and clean up the school." We saw an army of workmen busy replacing the windows of our classrooms, aided by bright spotlights.

Mr Fazeli was back in view. "We will work throughout the night," he said with great determination. "Tomorrow, our school will be open again as usual. We don't want the children to miss any more classes."

"Phew, what a relief," Mum said.

There was a soundtrack and a picture of the globe. Katie reappeared, smiling. "Well, now I'd like to introduce you to the richest dog in the world. For breakfast Bella Minella is served half a lobster every day. She then visits a fancy hairdresser who looks after her fur and once a week, Bella has an appointment at a beauty parlour to have her nails painted."

"Oh, so cute!" Lottie called out.

Dad switched the television off. "Pfff. So they're back at school tomorrow. Shame."

"Yes, Dad," I said. "What a shame for you, now you have to top up the nut trays all by yourself."

After tea I went upstairs. The clouds had gone, the sky was clear. I opened the curtains and looked at the stars. The longer I looked, the more I saw. Maybe I'd even spot a shooting star. You never knew. Hang on.

What if... there was another meteorite on its way. Perhaps it would smash into the loft window. Maybe I should move my bed to the other side of the room...

There was a knock on the door. Probably Lottie, thinking that I was making too much noise. "Go away!" I called out. The door opened slightly and Uncle Jack peeped in.

"I've brought you something," he said.

"Oh!" I said. "I didn't know it was you."

"Are you reorganizing your bedroom?" he asked.

"No, not really," I said, and I tried to push my bed back in place without him noticing, which was tricky.

"Look." Uncle Jack pulled out a box from behind his back. "I thought you could do with this."

WOOHOO! A real telescope! I have a REAL telescope! A proper one! Well, it is pretty old; it belonged to Uncle Jack when he was young, so not the very best telescope in the world, but still! "Can we try it out?" I asked.

"Of course," Uncle Jack said. We went downstairs and into the back garden. Uncle Jack carefully put up the telescope and explained in detail how to focus the lens. We looked at the moon and could see its craters and mountains. It was just awesome. I was still feeling a little bit worried about the events earlier in the day, so I casually asked my uncle what the chances were of a meteorite landing on our roof. He reassured me, saying it was very unlikely. "But it has happened," he said, and told me about all the terrible meteorites that had crashed into our planet. One meteorite was nearly ten kilometres wide and it caused nearly all dinosaurs to become extinct. When Uncle Jack had left, I moved my bed back to the other side of the room, but that was just because I fancied a change.

DOT-TO-DOT DRAWING

Do you want to do a spot of star gazing? A telescope is awesome. But amazingly, even with a pair of binoculars you can see a lot.

The Earth rotates and that's why the stars seem to move around in the night sky.
Go to tinyurl.com/greattimelapse or scan the code, for a cool video.

Stargazing isn't made easier by the fact that the stars are never in the same place as the night before. That's why, a long time ago, people mapped the sky like a dot-to-dot drawing. If you join the dots, you get a bear. Or a lion. Or a giraffe. Or a little fox. A water snake. A bull.

A group of stars like that – a constellation – is easy to spot. Once you've learned this skill, it can come in really handy. Like when you're stuck in the desert at night without a mobile phone or compass. If the sky is cloudless, you simply look up and find a group of stars that make up a frying pan. Extend the right end of the pan upward until you reach a very bright star. This is Polaris, the Pole Star or North Star. Polaris is always in the north. Hey presto – now you know where to go!

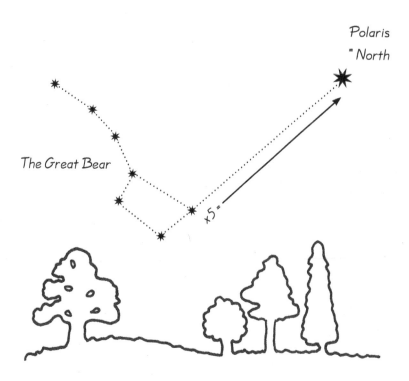

Polaris
= North

The Great Bear

x5 =

SKY MAP

A sky map is a map of the star-filled night sky. It teaches you how to recognize constellations. You can buy a sky map, or find one online. Want to have a look at tonight's sky? For an online UK sky chart visit: http://astronomynow.com/uk-sky-chart/

WANDERING STARS

You can also see planets at night. Planets look like stars, but they're not in a fixed place between the other stars because they rotate around the sun. As their movements seem random, planets used to be called "wandering stars". Visit an online sky map and you can see where the planets will be tonight.

WEDNESDAY

We went back to school today and I had to walk. "It's not fair," I said.

"It's bonkers," Lottie added.

"It's good for you!" Mum said, as she pulled her apron out of a drawer. "I used to walk to school every day. We also had our lunch at home so I had to do the walk twice in one day!"

"Ten kilometres," said Dad. "Those were the days. Come rain, come shine. In thunderstorms and downpours. In tatty old shoes. With holes in…" Mum tried to slap Dad, but he grabbed her hand and kissed it.

"Dad!" Lottie cried. "Please… don't!"

"Pease don't," Simon echoed, bashing his spoon against his porridge bowl.

"Yesterday we weren't even allowed to walk home by ourselves," I said.

"Well, I officially give you permission to walk to school on your own. And back. Shall I write a note for the teacher?" It was a TWENTY-minute walk to school.

The playground looked odd. There was a gaping hole where the shed had been. "We could make a pond," said Archie.

"Or a swimming pool," Christy suggested. "We just need to make it a bit bigger. Epic. A pool in the playground!"

"Then we can go ice skating in winter!" I said.

"Where do we leave our scooters and bikes?" asked Rachid.

"Where ARE the bikes?" said Matteo.

"Oh, I know," I said, and I ran off, ahead of everyone else, to the chestnut tree, where we'd moved them to last night.

"Whaaat?!" Archie cried out. "Look at my handlebars! Completely twisted!"

"My basket is ruined!" Christy said.

"My bell has gone!" Matteo added. "And my light is broken."

"Oh no. Really?" Rachid said angrily. "Look at my bike. The chain has come off and my tyres are flat! Wow. Happy days."

"It's not my fault, is it!?" I said.

"Did I say that?" Rachid replied, huffily.

The broken windows of our classroom had been replaced with safety glass, and the broken glass from yesterday had been swept away.

"Well, we all had a massive fright yesterday, didn't we?" Mr Nolan said. He sat down on a tall stool in our classroom. "It was a shock for us teachers. We didn't know what had happened."

"I wasn't frightened," Martin said. "I wasn't at all shocked."

"Nor me," said Tom. "I thought it was really cool. Fireworks, just like bonfire night!"

"I wasn't scared either," Matteo said.

"Oh, come on," said Luke. "You fell off your chair, Dumbo!"

"It was the impact of the crash," said Matteo, defensively. "I was BLOWN off my chair."

"Oh yeah. Sure!" Tom said.

"I was!"

"I was frightened by the whole thing," Christy said.

"Me too," Anna added. "I was bleeding. Look." She raised her hand, but there was no trace of blood, just a plaster.

"I couldn't sleep last night," Florence said. "I kept thinking, what if our house is hit by a meteorite?"

"Same for me!" Christy called out.

"This was just a small one," I said. "Once there was a meteorite that hit Mexico. It was so gigantic that it killed all the dinosaurs. And a few years ago, a meteorite came down in Russia and a thousand people were injured."

Florence raised her hand. "Sir, I think it's scary."

"And in 1908, a meteorite flattened the trees in Siberia," I added.

Florence stuck her fingers in her ears, shut her eyes, and sang loudly, "La la la la."

"And all the reindeer were killed."

"LA LA LA LA LA!" shouted Florence.

"Maybe we should change the subject and do something else, to distract us," Mr Nolan suggested.

"Play catch on the playground," Matteo suggested.

"Screen time!" Archie said. "Computers are a great distraction. Or the Wii."

"Sausage rolls," I chipped in. "A snack really helps when you need distraction."

"What about PE? The climbing wall?" Mr Nolan asked.

"YEEEEAAAH!" everyone shouted, except me. We went to the hall and Mr Nolan uncovered the climbing wall. He set out an obstacle course too, with benches, hoops, and ladders. He told me to go first. I hate climbing walls and obstacle courses.

All day we did unplanned activities. We spent some time drawing what we had seen the day before – "to process our feelings" as Mr Nolan put it. (I drew a dinosaur flattened by a meteorite.) We were allowed to read comics and we watched the film *Gnomeo and Juliet* after our lunch break.

Ten minutes left until home time.

"Can we leave early, Sir?" Archie asked. "To do some more processing?"

"No, I can't let you do that," Mr Nolan said. "I have to talk to you all first. I wanted to do this yesterday, but we uh, were hit by, uh, you know. Well, it just didn't happen. So, I've got this really awesome idea that we can do over the next few weeks. It's called 'a people library'."

Archie and I looked at each other.

"What?" I said.

"A people library."

"A place where we can borrow people?" Matteo chuckled.

"Epic!" Martin shouted. "I'll borrow a millionaire!"

In my head I pictured a library with lots of people next to each other on shelves. Some were high up; you needed a ladder to reach them.

But then the teacher said: "Of course it's not a real library. A people library means that you borrow interesting people for an hour or so. They come to school to tell us about something they know all about, like uh…" Mr Nolan frowned and looked at the ceiling. "… well, for instance, the Himalayas. Or Einstein. Or hot-air balloons."

Archie's hand shot up. "Sir! Can we have Steve Backshall or Bear Grylls?" Archie loves adventures and deadly creatures, especially crocodiles and snakes. He has a corn snake which he feeds dead mice.

"That would be fantastic," Mr Nolan said. "But perhaps we can find someone locally first. Who has a parent who can share an interesting story?"

"Me!" Rachid shouted. "My dad is a refugee. He came in a lorry and on a ferry!"

"That would be brilliant!" said Mr Nolan. "Do you think he'd be happy to come and talk to us?"

Rachid frowned. "Hmm, I'm not sure."

"My dad is a firefighter," Luke called. "It's really awesome. He puts out fires and last week he broke a window to rescue someone. On the third floor."

"My mum tests poo in the hospital!" Matteo shouted.

"Yuck!" Florence shrieked. Christy covered her eyes. Anna groaned. "How gross is that?"

"How does she test the poo?" Martin asked.

I wanted to know that, too. "Yes, how does she do it, actually? Does she use a gas mask? And gloves? Is it human or dog poo?"

Mr Nolan raised his hand. "Hang on! Let's pause here. Let's all have a think first about who we can invite. OK? This is going to be really exciting. We could borrow one or two grown-ups every week."

"Sir," I asked. "Does it have to be a parent? Can it be another relative? An uncle, maybe?"

"Of course," Mr Nolan said, "that's fine with me."

"My uncle knows everything about meteorites."

From: Sam Billington
To: Uncle Jack
Subject: People library

Hi Uncle Jack,

Thanks a million for the fab telescope. It works brilliantly – even if it's rusty and scratched. I've just spotted Mars, and Saturn's rings.

Quick question. My teacher wants to start up a people library. It means our class brings in people who have something interesting to share. If our parents have boring jobs, we're allowed to ask someone else. Could you please come and tell us all about meteorites?

Mum says you are very busy but please remember Granny's birthday!

Cheers, from Sam

From: Professor Jack Scott McNeil
To: Sam Billington
Subject: Re: People library

Dear Sam,

I'm thrilled you managed to spot Saturn's rings! Well done! I remember the first time I saw them (in Granny's back garden). It was totally awesome. Have you spotted Jupiter's moons? One thing to try out is to follow their movements for a few days and see how much their positions change (as they rotate around Jupiter, of course).

About your question: yes, I'd be delighted to do a talk for your people library. Next week I'm in Cambridge but I'm back on Friday and I could squeeze in a visit to your class then. Let me know if your teacher is up for that. I can tell you all about meteorites and our amazing universe.

All the best,
Uncle Jack

PS: Tell your Mum that yes, I'm very busy but I have managed to arrange a birthday present for Granny.

"WHAT?!" Mum exclaimed. "Why didn't you ask *me*?"

Sigh. "Muuum! Please. We only borrow interesting people."

"What did you say Uncle Jack had bought for Granny?"

From: Sam Billington
To: Uncle Jack
Subject: Re: People library

Hi Uncle Jack,

Please could you come EARLY on Friday, at 9-ish, so we can skip PE?

Mum asks what exactly you got for Granny. No skydiving please!

From: Professor Jack Scott McNeil
To: Sam Billington
Subject: Re: People library

Dear Sam,

Excellent – I'll be there!

See you on Friday,
Uncle Jack

PS: Please tell your Mum not to worry about Granny's birthday! I've organized a wild-bird safari from a nice comfortable boat.

FRIDAY MORNING

Yesssss! Uncle Jack is coming to our class today. That means we don't have PE! I hate PE and ESPECIALLY the climbing wall, cause I don't have enough strength in my arm muscles. And today is the day when we're supposed to do the climbing wall for our assessment. Bah.

Nooooo! Uncle Jack misread my email! He didn't turn up first thing this morning, so we DID have PE and had to go on the climbing wall after all. Mr Nolan watched us from below, taking notes. "Once you've got to the top and you've touched the ceiling, you can come back down and return to the changing rooms!" he called out.

Luke came down at top speed. "How are you getting on?" he asked me.

I rubbed my hands together. "Fine, thanks," I said. "I'm just warming up first."

He sniggered. "I bet you a bag of sweets that you won't even get halfway up the wall."

Mr Nolan clapped his hands. "Come on, come on! We haven't got all day!"

"Yeah, come on, you geek," Tom said. "Just get up there."

"AAAAARGHH!" A loud scream came from the girls' changing rooms.

"HEEEEELP!" shrieked Christy. "Sir, please come, it's the biggest spider EVER!"

Mr Nolan ran to the changing rooms and Tom and Luke followed.

"Quick!" Archie shouted. "Get onto my shoulders." Archie held out his hands so I could step onto them (which was quite tricky) and then climb onto his shoulders. I grabbed the climbing wall and nearly slipped off.

"Quick, get your feet onto the wall," cried Archie. "I can't hold you!"

I got myself onto the wall and looked down. I was a really long way up. But the ceiling was even further away. I looked up and stabilized myself. Mr Nolan came back in and I slowly moved down. My head was throbbing.

"What was that, Sir?" Archie asked.

Mr Nolan shrugged. "Oh, just a little spider." He looked at me and took some notes. "Get yourselves changed now."

When we were doing geography after playtime, there was a knock on the door. My head shot up. Was that...? Mr Nolan opened the door. Yes! It was him! My Uncle Jack! He came into the classroom with a holdall and a basketball in his arms.

"Who is that?" Luke asked.

"This is Professor Jack Scott McNeil," Mr Nolan said.

"WOOOOW," Martin said. "Jack Scott from High School Musical! He's on TV!"

"Not THAT Jack Scott," I said. "Professor Jack Scott – he's a scientist, not a singer."

"Professor Jack Scott is Sam's uncle and he's come for the people library," Mr Nolan said.

"So, do you do experiments with explosives?" Matteo asked. "I once did the one with a mint in a bottle of cola, and then..."

"You look more like a basketball player," said Mehmet.

"I thought all scientists wore white lab coats," said Esther. "And had glasses, and a moustache."

"Oh yes, and they have crazy hair!" shouted Matteo. "Wavy white hair, I mean, just over the ears and bald on top."

Uncle Jack laughed and put his basketball on Mr Nolan's desk. "Sorry to be such a disappointment, guys. But I've come straight from a match. That's why I don't look like a scientist."

"So, Professor Jack Scott Mc—" Mr Nolan continued.

"Please, just call me Jack," Uncle Jack chipped in.

"All right, Professor Jack is an astronomer. He's going to tell us all about meteorites."

Anna stared at Uncle Jack, with her elbows on her desk, cupping her hands around her chin. "Are you married?" she asked.

"Nope," replied Uncle Jack.

Anna smiled. "My mum isn't either."

Uncle Jack cleared his throat. "Right," he said. "So today, we're going to talk about the meteorite that landed on your bike and scooter shed."

"Yes!" Archie said in a huff. "My handlebars are completely crooked!"

"And my bell was ripped off!" Matteo added. "And my light is all messed up!"

"Your light never worked," Rachid said.

"Well, of course that's all very inconvenient," said Uncle Jack. "But at least we can be grateful that it wasn't as big as the meteorite that hit Russia, because—"

I coughed and tried to attract Uncle Jack's attention.

"What's the matter?" Uncle Jack said. "Are you OK?"

"Fine," I said, and I gestured at Uncle Jack to come over. I whispered: "You have to be careful; Florence was really traumatized by the whole thing."

"Aha," Uncle Jack whispered, and quickly changed the subject. "Let's talk about the universe," he said cheerfully.

"When the universe came into being, it was tiny," he started. "Even smaller than a speck of dust that you might see drifting in the sunlight. Millions of times smaller than a speck of dust."

"Could you grab it?" Archie asked. He was scribbling down everything Uncle Jack was saying. "The universe?"

Uncle Jack shook his head. "No. It was far too hot. The tiny universe was hotter than a thousand suns put together. And it was heavy. Heavier than an elephant. Heavier than a house."

"As heavy as the world?" Christy asked.

Uncle Jack laughed. "Much heavier. That one tiny speck of dust was as heavy as all the stars and planets together."

"No way!" Matteo called out. "That is SUPER mega heavy!"

"And then," Uncle Jack continued, "this tiny speck of dust exploded with the biggest explosion ever: the Big Bang. The teeny-weeny baby universe erupted and transformed within a fraction of a second into a gigantic space, even bigger than the Milky Way. Our universe had been born. Time had started. Space had started."

"And when was this?" enquired Archie. He was about to write down the answer.

"Almost 14 billion years ago," Uncle Jack answered. Tom and Luke stared at each other.

"Pfff," said Tom. "That's impossible."

"How do you know?" Luke chipped in. "Were you there watching?"

They're so rude, these guys, especially when talking to a GUEST. Who happens to be my UNCLE. And a PROFESSOR. But Uncle Jack didn't mind the rudeness. He was passionate.

"Yes, isn't that incredible? The universe is just like a video you can rewind. Hang on, let me show you!" He fished around in his pockets. "Hmm, where is it?" he muttered. "I'm sure I brought it."

"Have you lost something?" asked Christy.

"A balloon," Uncle Jack replied.

"A balloon?" Tom and Luke grinned at each other.

I started to feel slightly nervous. Uncle Jack looked so distracted. Maybe he'd been hit by a basketball during his match.

"Where IS it?" Uncle Jack rummaged through all his pockets and then, "Aha." Out of his back pocket he pulled a blue balloon. He blew it up a little, took a felt-tip pen and marked it with dots. "These are stars," he said. "And what happens, do you think, if I keep blowing up the balloon?"

"Don't you know that yourself?" Tom remarked.

Mr Nolan cleared his throat and gave Tom a telling look.

"Pfff. Well. I mean, it's obvious, it'll burst," Tom said. Uncle Jack started to blow. The balloon grew bigger and bigger.

"The stars are moving apart!" Florence shouted.

Uncle Jack stopped blowing and tied a knot in the balloon. "Spot on!" he said. "The stars that were close together a minute ago are now further apart. And that is exactly what is happening in our universe. Galaxies are moving away from each other. The universe is getting bigger and bigger all the time, and we can measure exactly at what speed it is expanding. This is useful because it enables us to calculate back to when it all started with the one tiny speck, basically by rewinding the sequence."

"The Big Bang," Archie said.

Uncle Jack nodded. "Indeed. The Big Bang."

"What?!" Anna called out. "The Big Bang is a fairy tale, isn't it? Made up by people who don't believe in God!"

"Actually, no, that's not the case," Uncle Jack replied, and he began to describe to us how in the beginning the Earth was a big mess, with bits of rock crashing into it. A mega collision split the Earth into two. "One part of the Earth became our moon." Florence stared out of the window, looking increasingly worried. "And 65 million years ago," Uncle Jack continued, "a rock that was nearly ten kilometres wide fell onto the Earth."

"TEN kilometres!" Matteo exclaimed. "That's a two-hour walk!"

"And that's when dinosaurs became extinct."

Florence raised her hand. She looked pale. "Mr Nolan? I'm not feeling well."

COLLIDING ROCKS

 There are still lumps of rock drifting around in space. In 2014 a mini rocket even managed to land on a comet; you can watch it here: tinyurl.com/rosettatouchdown and www.esa. int/esatv/Videos/2014/11/Rosetta_landing_ on_a_comet or scan the code!

Do you think another gigantic meteorite could hit our planet? Fortunately, the chances are very small. Our atmosphere protects the Earth from falling pieces of rock. You'd have thought that a meteorite could easily fall through the thin air of the atmosphere, but meteorites are so INCREDIBLY fast, they heat up so much that by the time they reach the Earth they're often burnt up. (Shooting stars are the result; you may have seen them in the night sky.)

Very occasionally, things go wrong. In 2013, a huge meteorite hit Russia. It was over 16 metres wide! Before entering our atmosphere, it exploded in the sky and a trail of fire was visible

 from the Earth. The debris came down at nearly 18 kilometres per second. Many people were injured because of broken glass and shattered windows. See: tinyurl.com/meteorhitsrussia or scan the code.

Space agencies are trying to detect any lumps of rock from space that may cause problems in the future. One day, they hope to find a way to steer those rocks in the opposite direction, away from the Earth.

THE METEORITE THAT WIPED OUT THE DINOSAURS

Sixty-five million years ago, near Mexico, an enormous 10-kilometre-wide meteorite hit the Earth. The impact was huge, about 2 million times bigger than the explosion of the largest nuclear bomb!

The meteorite went right into the Earth and caused huge vibrations, sparking off tsunamis and horrible earthquakes all over the world. Melted rocks were catapulted into the sky and hot, glowing lumps of stone rained down onto the Earth. An enormous amount of dust was blown into the sky, which meant that the sun couldn't be seen for months. This led to a massive drop in temperature and the Earth became a freezing cold place. Plants and trees died out because of the lack of sunlight. Many animal species became extinct, including the vast majority of dinosaurs. The vegetarian dinosaurs that had survived the catastrophe couldn't find anything to eat, so they died. What about the meat-eaters that were still around?
They had the same problem, and so they died too. The only types of dinosaur that survived were the flying ones. You can see their great-great-great-great-grandchildren frolicking around in your garden.

THE BEGINNING OF PLANET EARTH

Have you ever looked under your bed? If you don't vacuum very often, you'll find some clumps of dust. Small bits of dust and hair that end up on the floor move upwards when there's a bit of wind. When you open a door, for instance. If they collide, they'll stick together. That's why it's easy to pick up lumps of dust and throw them in the bin (or blow them out of the window).

Very old stars stop burning and explode. This way, gas and dust and debris are catapulted into space. These lumps begin to swirl around and very slowly, they start sticking together. The sun was formed when very cold clouds of gas and dust came together.

When this enormous mass reached a certain size, it began to heat up. Around the sun, there were lots of small planets. The planets couldn't stick to their orbits and instead, they became more like dodgem cars crashing into each other. Eventually, thanks to gravity, they melted together into a bigger planet.

This is how, nearly 5 billion years ago, our planet Earth came into being. Our planet is, in fact, nothing more than a massive lump of waste. It's made up of the debris of exploded stars! It's brilliant recycling!

THE BIGGEST BANG

How loud was the Big Bang? The Big Bang was DEAD silent! That's because sound is made up of vibrations. As there wasn't anything to shake around yet at that point, there weren't any vibrations. The biggest bang in history was also the quietest!

Then the bell went off.

"Wow!" exclaimed Mr Nolan. "That was extremely interesting. Do you really have to go already?"

"Can't you come back after lunch break?" asked Christy.

"Yes, please!" Archie called out. "You're much more fun than our teacher."

"We've learned so much today," Rachid added.

"Thanks very much, you're a very kind bunch," said Mr Nolan.

Uncle Jack looked at his watch. "Well, I could maybe stay for another hour, if you'd like me to."

"Who would like Professor Jack to stay on for a bit?" asked Mr Nolan. "Even if it means missing your lunch break?"

Tom slumped back in his chair. "I'd rather have my lunch break."

"Me too," Luke said. "I want to play football."

"No, please don't go yet!" Christy chipped in. "You have to stay!"

"Yes, yes, STAY!" Archie shouted.

"All right then," Mr Nolan said. "Let's have five minutes outside to get some fresh air. All of you, go for a quick run around the playground. As it's a packed-lunch day, you can all eat in class while Professor Jack continues with his talk."

FRIDAY AFTERNOON

Five laps around the playground. That's what Mr Nolan usually tells Matteo to do when he's being too fidgety. But now we all had to go out and run five laps. I hate running, especially when I'm hungry. But, I thought, the sooner I finish, the sooner I can be back for my packed lunch, so I ran as fast as I could. It was going well. I was faster than all the girls (except Christy).

"Hey!" Matteo shouted, when he overtook me. "Sam! Is this only your fourth lap? It's my fifth!" But as he was shouting, he knocked over a Reception child, who burst into tears. Miss Smith told Matteo to stop and say sorry. When he was back on track, I'd already finished. Wow. This was the first time EVER that I'd beaten Matteo. Awesome.

"Is everyone here?" Mr Nolan asked, when we were back in the classroom. "You're allowed to start eating your packed lunches here today, if you promise not to make any noise. Professor Jack is going to talk to us about... uhmm..."

"... the universe," Uncle Jack said. "Has anyone here ever been on a far-away holiday?"

"We have!" Archie said. "To France!"

"Spain!" shouted Luke. He looked smug and took a bite of his cheese sandwich. He thought he'd been further than anyone else, but Rachid had been to Turkey. Too bad for Luke.

"Turkey," Uncle Jack said. "That is really far."

"REALLY far!" Rachid echoed proudly. "We were in the car for thirty hours. We only stopped five times, just for a wee."

"And a poo?" Matteo checked.

"Of course. But that was all."

Uncle Jack scratched his head. I don't think they talk about wee and poo in his lab as often as we do in our class. "Right, yes, Turkey is very far away indeed. But even if you're in Turkey you're not even halfway across the globe. Nothing like halfway, actually.

If you drive 1,000 kilometres per day, it will take you nearly 40 days to go around the Earth. But if, on the way home, you drive east rather than west, you gain a day. That means you could return in 39 days instead!

Imagine motorways across the oceans, so you could drive around the entire Earth. How long would it take you? Any guesses?"

I raised my hand. "One week?"

Uncle Jack shook his head. "Forty days!"

"Forty days?" said Christy. She put her water bottle down. "Forty days in the car? With my little brother? No way!"

I turned to look at Christy. She's pretty awesome (for a girl). I wouldn't mind travelling round the world for forty days with Christy next to me. But I couldn't bear the thought of sitting in between Simon and Lottie for that long. Two hours in the car next to snotty Simon is as much as I can take.

"And imagine," Uncle Jack carried on, "that you wanted to travel to the sun. Do you know how long that would take, if you went by car and didn't stop at all? A hundred and seventy-one years!"

"You can't drive a car through the sky!" Archie said.

"No, of course not," Uncle Jack admitted. "A car is difficult to drive off the road. It would be better to go by rocket. That would take just over three months. The sun is really, really far away. And the Earth is tiny."

Uncle Jack bent down and picked a breadcrumb off the floor. "Look," he said, holding the crumb between his thumb and index finger. "This is the Earth..."

It wouldn't be very clever to travel to the sun, because it's extremely hot there. On the outside of the sun it's 6,000 degrees Celsius. And there are jet flames of over a million kilometres high! If you got near one of those, you and your rocket would be roasted in no time.

"No way," said Tom. "That's a breadcrumb."

"All right. It is a breadcrumb. But imagine it was the Earth." Uncle Jack picked his basketball off the desk and bounced it up and down a few times. "This is the sun. The Earth fits into the sun more than a million times. It is that big. But the sun is actually quite a small star."

Uncle Jack went on to tell us about stars that were much, much bigger than the sun. Like Arcturus, and Canis Major, which is so enormous that to fly around it by plane would take you 787 years! Some stars are so far away that you would never manage to get there. Compared to them, the sun wasn't that far away, he told us, but to reach the star closest to the sun by rocket would take you 81,000 years.

"You'd need to go with a lot of people," said Rachid.

Uncle Jack scratched his head and looked a bit worried.

The sun is 150 million kilometres away. How long would it take you to get there?

- *157 days taking the fastest rocket*
- *171 years by car*
- *684 years on horseback*
- *1,140 years on a bike*
- *3,420 years on foot*

"And they'd need to get married and have kids, who would need to get married and have kids, and so on," Rachid continued.

"That wouldn't be possible!" Mehmet chipped in. "The older people would die – what would you do with them?"

"You would throw them out of the rocket," Matteo said, beaming. "So they would float around in space for ever!"

"Frozen," I said.

"Zombies in space!" Martin shouted.

"Not for me, thank you very much," Christy said, as she folded her arms. "No way would I join you."

"Me neither," I quickly said.

Uncle Jack explained how fast light travels and that you can go back in time, finding out how many stars there are.

Suddenly, he glanced at his watch and called out: "I need to go now!" and he ran out of the classroom.

"That was so epic," Christy sighed.

"Sir," Matteo asked. "May I go for a run now?"

AT THE SPEED OF LIGHT

The longer you observe the night sky, the more stars you'll be able to see. You actually need about half an hour for your eyes to get used to the dark, and once they are you'll see more and more stars. Without a telescope you can see nearly 5,000 stars. But this is only possible if you're in a dark place, without street light.

In the United Kingdom, there are some very dark areas left, which are hotspots for star gazing. See: www.nationaltrust. org.uk/features/top-spots-for-stargazing and www. darkskydiscovery.org.uk/dark-sky-discovery-sites/map.html

Stars look really tiny, but that's because they're extremely far away. We don't calculate distance to the stars in kilometres or by working out how many years it would take you to get there in a rocket. We use the speed of light. Light can travel really fast: nearly 300,000 kilometres per second. That is mega fast: nearly eight laps around the Earth in one second! It takes sunlight eight minutes to reach you. When you see the sun setting into the sea on holiday, the sun actually went down eight minutes earlier. Imagine that the sun exploded right NOW. You would only see it in eight minutes' time. The light of the Proxima Centauri takes four years to reach Earth. If someone switched off the light now, you would only notice in four years' time! And, in fact, the Proxima Centauri is not that far away. If you look at the stars at night, you look much further back in time. You can see what certain stars looked like ten years ago, or one hundred years, or even four thousand years.

TIME MACHINE

Have you ever watched a film about people travelling back to prehistoric times? Sadly, we don't have time machines yet, to try it out for real. Imagine, though, that you could watch the Earth from the stars, with a very powerful telescope...

- Sirius is one of the brightest stars in the night sky. It takes more than eight years for light to travel from the Earth to Sirius. From Sirius they would be able to watch you walking around as a toddler. (That would of course only work if people could go to stars – which they can't!)
- The sun-like Kepler-11 star is 2,000 light years away! From Kepler-11 you would be able to see Jesus walking around in Israel. You could watch his parents looking for him when he was a boy, and watch him talking to religious teachers at the Temple. You could even watch him calm a storm from a little boat!
- From a star that is 65 million light years away, you could take photos of dinosaurs. With a bit of luck you would see the gigantic meteorite crash into Mexico.
- From a star that is 4 billion light years away, you would be able to observe how the Earth was just a lump of bits of debris stuck together, hit by meteorites.

BIG!

The stars you see at night are the stars of the Milky Way: our very own galaxy, with lots and lots of stars. One hundred billion, in fact. Do you know how long it takes to count to one billion? Thirty-two years! You would need to count non-stop for 3,200 years to count all the stars in the Milky Way alone...

The Milky Way is one of many galaxies in the universe. We've already discovered 100 million other galaxies, some much *bigger than ours and all with billions of stars.*

It is totally mind blowing, dazzling. The universe is unimaginably, immeasurably, incredibly large. And it's getting bigger all the time.

From: Sam Billington
To: Uncle Jack
Subject: Basketball

Hi Uncle Jack,

Our class really enjoyed your visit. Thank you for taking part in our people library. Did you know you left your basketball behind? I think you'll need to come back another time to collect it. And by the way, we still have lots and lots of questions for you.

Also, I must ask you this question. You told us that there was a super collision and that the Earth split in two, into a moon and planet Earth. But then why is the Earth a globe and not half a sphere? And what about the moon?

Cheers,
Sam

From: Professor Jack Scott McNeil
To: Sam Billington
Subject: Re: Basketball

Dear Sam,

Thanks for your message. I thought it was wonderful to come and tell you and your classmates all about the universe. You asked so many great questions! And no, you wouldn't end up with two half spheres (even if it may look like that when it's a half moon). If you bashed two watermelons against each other, they'd smash into dozens of little bits. This is sort of what happened during the collision. But those floating pieces were pulled back together by gravity, and this is how the Earth and the moon were formed. Over time, gravity pulled all those loose pieces closely together and formed two perfect spheres that spin around each other.

Best wishes,
Uncle Jack

From: Sam Billington
To: Uncle Jack
Subject: Re: Basketball

Oh yes, I also wanted to ask you this: do you know why so many ships disappear in the Bermuda Triangle?

From: Professor Jack Scott McNeil
To: Sam Billington
Subject: Re: Basketball

That's a myth. On average, no more ships disappear in the Bermuda Triangle than anywhere else in the world where navigation is difficult and violent tropical storms cause problems... but people just love to believe in mysterious forces and conspiracy theories.

Best wishes,
Uncle Jack

SATURDAY

I woke up this morning with Lottie squeezing my nose. She had come into my room! My room is strictly forbidden territory for girls, and especially sisters. I pushed her away.

"What are you doing here!" I shouted. "Go away!"

"Archie is here."

I looked at my alarm clock. It was half past seven. Half past seven on SATURDAY!

"Do you think you're being funny?" I said, turning over. "Go away!"

"Hi Sam." Archie entered the room and sat down on the far end of my bed. He looked incredibly awake. "Are you ready for this?"

"For what?!"

"For the annual Great British Beach Clean, Dumbo!" Archie replied, excitedly. "We have to get there early. The earlier we get there, the more rubbish we can collect!"

"What? I've never made any mess on the beach. Why do I need to clean it up?" I groaned.

"Just put on some shorts," said Archie. "And wellies."

I pulled the duvet over my head. "I'm not going. Didn't you hear me?"

Archie opened my wardrobe.

"Hey, watch out!" I called, but it was too late. All my clothes came falling out, as well as a stack of comics, a rabbit skull, a bag of peanuts... And my very best fossils tumbled down off the top shelf.

"Ouch!" Archie cried out.

"Watch what you're doing!" I jumped out of bed and dived onto the floor. "My fossils!"

Archie limped towards my bed and checked his foot. "I could have broken my foot thanks to your rotten stones, Dumbo!"

"And that would have been your own stupid fault. You loser! You shouldn't just open someone else's wardrobe! They could have smashed to pieces! Oh no. My rabbit skull!"

"Sam!" Mum came into the room wearing a pink flowery dressing gown. "How lovely that you're taking part in the beach clean. What on earth happened here? Why are there peanuts on the floor?"

"It was Archie's fault," I said. "He wants me to wade through the mud. No way. Look at my poor rabbit skull!"

"Of course you must go," Mum said. "A bit of exercise won't harm you. Chop chop. Get your clothes on."

I fished the bits of rabbit skull out from among the scattered peanuts. It would take me hours to put the skull back together. "I'm really not coming. You go on your own."

But fifteen minutes later Archie and I sat in the back of his mum's car, on our way to the beach. We had to climb some dunes, and my wellies (actually my mum's boots, which were far too big for me) nearly slipped off. I was NOT happy. But then all of a sudden I heard Christy's voice.

"Hey Sam! Are you helping out, too?"

"Of course!" I said. I quickly bent over to dig a plastic bottle out of the sand, but not before I noticed that today she had hundreds of really cool black plaits with small, colourful beads. "I'm all for cleaning up the beach. And for the environment and so on."

"Me too!" Christy said cheerfully.

All of a sudden the day seemed a bit brighter.

Within two hours I had collected:
- Six bits of fishing net
- 18 plastic bottles
- A rusty trike
- A green welly, size 11

I had to wade through the water to get to the welly, as it was stuck in a mud bank. With hindsight, that was a bad idea. The water looked shallow, but there was actually a deep hole in the bottom. As I went in, the water came up to my middle. Archie tried to pull me out, but my left welly had got sucked into the mud. Instead of stepping out of the hole, I fell forward and got completely soaked. When I got back up again, I was only wearing one welly. And it was full of water.

"Why did you get in there in the first place? That water is nearly 2 metres deep," Archie said.

"It isn't my fault that there was a hole in the bottom!" I said, feeling really frustrated. "I could have drowned! All because you just had to clean up the beach!"

Christy came running over, her plastic carrier bag bouncing up and down. "Sam! What happened?"

"Nothing," I said swiftly. "I just wanted to test how deep it was."

Archie probably realized it was all his fault, as he offered to search for my welly. Then, all of a sudden, I spotted something far more interesting. A black thing that was only half visible. I pulled it out of the mud. It looked like a bone. A round bone, with lots of bits sticking out. A kind of monster with four legs and no head.

Archie had already opened his bin liner, but I said: "No, I'm taking this home."

"What is it?" Christy asked.

"A bone, I think. Perhaps it belongs to a seal. I'll add it to my collection."

"To your wardrobe collection, I bet." Archie took the bone from me and smelled it. He winced, and said: "I'm sure it's just a stone."

"I bet you a bag of sweets that it IS a bone," I said.

From: Sam Billington
To: contact@naturalhistorymuseum.org
Subject: Bone found

Hello.

I am sending you a photo of a bone. Please can you tell me what type of bone this is? I found it on the beach.

IMPORTANT: If this is not a bone, but a stone, please don't reply (or I will have to buy a bag of sweets for my friend Archie).

Best wishes,
Sam

From: Alice
To: Sam Billington
Subject: Re: Bone found

Hi Sam,

You can rest assured, you won't need to buy your friend Archie a bag of sweets. It is indeed a bone that you found. And a very interesting one, too! It looks like a joint of a woolly rhinoceros. This means that it is at least 40,000 years old. But it could even be 200,000 years old. You can send us the bone, so we can do some research on it.

Best wishes,
Alice

WOOHOOOO! A woolly rhino?

EPIC!!

My collection was becoming more amazing by the day. Even if my clothes did smell of fish.

MONDAY

When I arrived at school today, I noticed that Luke's dad was in our classroom. So was Esther's mum and Tom's mum. They were deep in conversation with Mr Nolan, and Esther's mum was energetically waving her arms around. Tom's mum had red blotches all across her neck and Luke's dad didn't sound too friendly.

"Are they all here for the people library?" I asked Archie.

He didn't know. I asked Christy, who didn't know either.

"I'll go and find out," I said. I got a tissue out of my pocket, pretended to blow my nose, and walked slowly to the bin, so I could get closer and work out what they were talking about.

"I am so shocked," Tom's mum said. "Completely shocked."

"I thought this was a Christian school!" Luke's dad chipped in.

"So did I," Esther's mum added. "I always assumed my children were safe here."

Whoops. What on earth had happened? Had Mr Nolan accidentally hit a child? Had a bike been stolen? Had someone tampered with the SATS tests?

"But then one day my son comes home and he's talking about the Big Bang," Tom's mum continued.

"Exactly!" Esther's mum said. "And saying that the universe is billions of years old, as if anyone has evidence for that."

"The Bible says clearly that God made everything! The entire universe and everything in it. Just like that, in six days! But along comes some kind of university professor who thinks he knows everything and who says, 'No, it didn't happen in six days, that's impossible; in fact it took 10 billion years'."

"Actually it was 13.8 billion," I murmured.

Tom's mum turned around. "What did you say, Sam?"

"I said it was 13.8 billion years. The Big Bang, that is. It wasn't 10 billion but *13.8 billion years* ago."

Tom's mum raised her eyebrows. "You see!" she shouted. "There you have it. Those poor children have taken this nonsense on board. If you told them that aliens from Mars had just landed on Earth, they would believe it too."

"No way!" I said. "If there's any life on Mars at all, it's just bacteria."

But no one was listening to me anymore.

"What's next? Apes are our ancestors? This professor would probably support that idea, don't you think?" Tom's mum continued.

"Well, he never mentioned that," Mr Nolan said. "But..."

Luke's dad raised his hand and butted in. "Great idea, Mr Nolan, to organize a people library, but please invite only those with sensible ideas to share."

"My mum will come and do a talk!" Anna said, when Mr Nolan had finally got rid of all the parents.

"Excellent," Mr Nolan said. "What would she like to talk about?"

"Horses."

Archie and I glanced at each other. Horses. Yuck. I wouldn't dream of inviting my mum to come in and tell the class about dry fermented salami or smelly French cheeses. But for some strange reason, the girls all cheered loudly. "Yeeeeaaah! Horses!"

"Cool!"

"When is she coming?"

"Will she bring a horse to school?"

"Great idea!" Mr Nolan said. "Ask her to come tomorrow!"

From: Sam Billington
To: Uncle Jack
Subject: Big Bang

Hi Uncle Jack,

You won't believe what happened in class today. Some of the parents came in to complain about your talk, especially what you said about the Big Bang (13.8 billion years ago). They said it's all rubbish, because God made the universe. Sorry Uncle Jack.

Cheers,
Sam

From: Professor Jack Scott McNeil
To: Sam Billington
Subject: Re: Big Bang

I'm so sorry to hear that some of the parents were upset. I actually don't think they have a reason to feel this way. I too believe that God made the universe, the Earth, and everything else. Thanks to our telescopes we've been able to discover that he created it 13.8 billion years ago. So I don't really understand why these parents are angry and upset, because I totally agree with them that God made the universe.

Best wishes,
Uncle Jack

TUESDAY

The day didn't get off to a great start. We'd run out of Cheerios and my experiment with vinegar and baking powder caused a little bit of chaos, when a cork popped into my eye and I dropped a glass bottle, which smashed into a thousand pieces on the kitchen floor. Mum didn't even feel sorry for me! In fact, she shouted: "Upstairs now and put some clean pants on!"

I had no idea why she wanted me to put some clean pants on. Until I got to the school gate and saw the school doctor's car. And then you know that at some point you will be asked to leave the classroom and go to the sick room, where you will need to get weighed in your boxers. And that the school doctor will tell you the same as she did the year before.

"I'm afraid you're at the top end of the healthy weight range."

This is doctor's speak for "you are FAT".

Really unsociable that an adult is allowed to say this to a child, just like that. It might cause me stress.

"Do you know how much I'd weigh if I was on Pluto?" I called from behind the curtain where I was getting changed.

"No idea," replied the doctor.

"Only 2.3 kilograms. Practically nothing!"

I opened the curtain. "By the way, on Pluto I'd also be much better at PE. I'd be able to jump a few metres high. I'd jump even higher than a kangaroo!"

"Well, yes," started the doctor, while she typed something on her laptop. "But you don't live on Pluto." And then she told me to do half an hour's exercise every day and that I should limit my screen time. It's a good thing I didn't start talking about Jupiter – I'd be nearly 83 kilograms there.

LIFE ON PLUTO IS LOUSY

a) You can't breathe so you need a spacesuit to survive.

b) -231 Celsius is freezing!

c) One day on Pluto is like six days on Earth. Head teachers would want to capitalize on that of course – no doubt we'd have eighty-hour school days! As if school was all that mattered.

d) It's quite hard to type and Skype when wearing a spacesuit.

e) The winds are extremely strong on Pluto. It'd be a great place for renewable energy.

f) There is almost no gravity – not great for children who are still growing. They would end up hunchbacked and severely deformed.

g) Pluto is a dwarf planet, it would be overpopulated at once.

As soon as I got back to my classroom, there was a knock on the door. It was Anna's mum. She had a blond ponytail, just like Anna, and was wearing a tight pair of jodhpurs and shiny riding boots. She was holding a whip in one hand and a riding cap in the other. She looked a bit like a grown-up version of a little girl and invited us to call her Louise.

"I've come here to tell you all about horses," Louise said. "And about riding schools and how to clean a horse shoe. But before I do all that, I want to briefly talk about what you heard earlier in the week, about the Big Bang."

"Yes!" Archie called out. "Hang on, let me just grab my notebook and pen!"

I raised my hand. "Could you please tell us a bit more about the moon, and how exactly it was formed? When the Earth was hit by a meteorite."

Louise shook her head, her ponytail swinging wildly. She raised her hand. "Hang on guys, that's not what I am going to talk about today. All I wanted to say was that I really hope none of you believe that the Big Bang really happened. OK? Because if you do, I will need to disappoint you. The Big Bang is a fairy tale."

What?

What did she just say?

"It's completely made up, by people who don't believe in God. They cooked up a theory about how the universe was formed. But this theory clashes with the Bible. You all know this. The Bible says that God made everything in six days. Here, let me write it down for you."

Day 1 Light
Day 2 Sky
Day 3 Dry land and sea, plants and trees
Day 4 The sun, moon, and stars
Day 5 Birds and fish
Day 6 Mammals and humans

I looked at the whiteboard and frowned. Something wasn't right.

How odd.

From my pre-school days I knew that God had made everything in six days, but only now *did* I see it.

I raised my hand. "Are you saying that the sun was made on day four?"

Louise nodded. "Yes, that's right."

"But what happened on the first three days? When the sun wasn't there yet, even though there was light?" I asked. "That's impossible, isn't it? How could there be light but no sun?"

"Duhhh!" Florence responded. "They just forgot to mention the sun on Day 1 – writing was quite an effort in those days. Quills, ink spills, scrolls and other dodgy paper."

I groaned. Girls.

"I can see Sam's point," Mr Nolan interrupted. "There was no sun during the first three days, but it was light during the daytime and dark at night. How is that possible?"

Phew, at least one person understood what I was trying to say.

"God can do everything," Louise responded. "So, he can easily provide light before he'd made the sun. That wouldn't have been a problem for him."

"But..." I gasped. I wanted to ask how long those first three days lasted if there was no sun to determine night and day – but instead I just yelped "Ouch" as I felt a very sharp and nasty sting in my bottom. Mr Nolan asked what was up, but I just said "Nothing". I knew that if I told him it was Luke, pressing the tip of his compass into my behind, it would backfire in break time.

"But the stars are extremely ancient!" Archie said. "A few billion years old, in fact."

I knew Archie wouldn't let me down.

But Louise had an answer for everything. "The stars do *seem* very old, but that doesn't mean that they really *are* that old. What did Adam look like when he was made, do you think?"

Esther guessed, "Twenty, maybe?"

"Or eighteen," Martin said. "I think it's eighteen."

"I think probably thirty-ish," Christy chipped in.

I nodded. Thirty. That was exactly what I thought.

"So, Adam didn't look like a baby?" Louise asked. I shook my head. No. Adam didn't look like a baby. I was sure of it. If he'd been a baby, he wouldn't have been walking around, chatting with God and naming the animals and so on.

"See?" Louise said. "Adam was only a few minutes old and he already looked twenty or thirty. And Eve as well. God gave both of them a body that looked much older. And that's exactly how he made the Earth. God created a ready-made world. It looked very old, but was, in fact, brand new. The stars look like they are old, billions of years perhaps, but that too is just how it appears. God made them look ancient."

"But how is it possible that we can see stars that are extremely far away?" I said. "If their light has been travelling for millions of years to reach the Earth, then those stars must be millions of years old too!"

"Or even billions of years," Archie added.

Louise shook her head. "God can arrange for the light that is millions or billions of light years away to reach the Earth in just one second."

I felt awful, as if I'd been tricked. And Louise just went on and on.

"Just imagine a dump with massive skips full of rubbish," she said. "Have you ever been to a dump?"

I nodded. I had been to one with Dad when we needed a headlight for our old Volvo. It was a jumbled mess. Pieces of iron and broken tyres, mouldy car seats and rusty hub-caps.

"All right," Louise said. "Imagine a tornado racing around the dump. A wild and terrible tornado. And then, as soon as the tornado has moved on, you find the area clear and clean, with the bits of scrap transformed into a Boeing 747. Flying engine included."

"Impossible!" Matteo shouted.

"Correct. It is impossible," Louise said. "If there's a tornado raging through a dump, the mess will only get worse. It wouldn't ever be possible for a Boeing to come out of all that. Do you really believe that out of a Big Bang stars and planets can be formed? And a world with plants and trees and air and people?! Impossible! And the Earth isn't that old at all," she went on. "At least not 4 billion years old. And we can prove it!"

"How?" I asked.

"Well, it's a little bit complicated," she said.

"That's not a problem," Mr Nolan said. "These children are all very intelligent."

Anna's mum nodded. "OK. Let me tell you a secret. There is a chemical element that we can use to find out how old something is. It's called carbon 14. Carbon 14 is part of every living thing. You can find it in trees. In plants."

"And in me?" asked Matteo.

"Yes, in you too."

"Where is it then?" Matteo studied his hands.

"We can talk about that another time. Now we're talking about plants and trees. When a plant or tree dies, carbon begins to break down. This happens very slowly. After nearly 6,000 years, only half of the carbon is left. After another 6,000 years, just a quarter of the original carbon is left. And after another 6,000 years, it's down to one eighth. After 100,000 years there is so little carbon left, you can't measure it any longer. Not even with the most sophisticated equipment."

Matteo fell off his chair.

"Matteo," Mr Nolan said. "Why don't you go for a run around the playground?"

"Can I go, too?" Florence asked.

"Am I getting a bit too complicated?" Louise asked.

"They ARE still listening," Mr Nolan said. "But some children find it easier to concentrate when they are able to go for a run around the block every now and again. They need the oxygen for their brains. Matteo, please close the door gentl—"

BAM!

Louise smiled. "Who knows what oil is made of?" she continued. "Or coal?"

"Plants and trees!" I replied.

"That's right! And do you also know how old oil and coal are?"

"A few hundred million years," I said, as I happened to know the answer.

Louise shook her head. "Hmm. Well. That's what the scientists think. They think it took hundreds of millions of years for those trees and shrubs to turn into oil and coal. So, if that's the case, do you think there'd still be any carbon 14 left in the oil and coal?"

I thought for a moment. Carbon is part of every living thing, but... "No, that's not possible. Because it's gone after 100,000 years."

"Well, this is the thing!" Louise said. "There IS carbon 14 in oil and coal. So, it can't be that old after all! And if oil and coal aren't that old, the Earth doesn't have to be that old either."

"In that case, how old IS the Earth?" Mr Nolan asked.

"Well, that's easy," Louise said. "You can just look it up in the Bible. If you can add and subtract, you can work it out for yourself."

God made Adam on the sixth day.
0
Adam became the father of Seth when he was 130 years old
0 + 130 = 130
Seth became the father of Enosh when he was 105 years old.
130 + 105 = 235
Enosh became the father of Cainan when he was 90 years old.
235 + 90 = 325
Cainan became the father of Mahalalel when he was 70 years old.
325 + 70 = 395
Mahalalel became the father of Jared when he was 65 years old.
395 + 65 = 460
Jared became the father of Enoch when he was 162 years old.
460 + 162 = 622
Enoch became the father of Methuselah when he was 65 years old.
622 + 65 = 687
Methuselah became the father of Lamech when he was 187 years old.
687 + 187 = 874

Lamech became the father of Noah when he was 182 years old.
874 + 182 = 1056
The flood happened when Noah was 600 years old.
1056 + 600 = 1656

Louise turned around. "And Jesus was born some 2,500 years later."

Archie had got his mobile phone out and was typing everything into his calculator. "So you think the Earth is 6,174 years old?" he asked.

Louise put down her whiteboard pen. "Yes, roughly."

There were footsteps in the corridor. The door flew open.

Matteo and Florence were back.

"Are we STILL not talking about horses?!" cried Florence.

"Yes!" said Esther. "You were going to tell us about horses!"

Louise laughed. "Oh yes," she said. "I nearly forgot!" She put on her riding helmet and pulled a USB stick from her trouser pocket. She gave it to Mr Nolan. "Could you put this in your laptop, please? Look. This is a horse and this is a pony. Did you know that Napoleon only wanted to ride on white horses? His favourite horse was called Marengo, and it lived until the age of thirty-eight. Horses have the biggest eyes of all mammals, but..."

A scrunched up piece of paper landed on my desk. I didn't know where it had come from, but I unfolded it. It said:

Now you know — your uncle doesn't have a **CLUE!** He's just as dumb as you are, you stupid geek!!

From: Sam Billington
To: Uncle Jack
Subject: 6,000 years

Hi Uncle Jack,

I'm totally confused. Today Anna's mum came to school and she said that first God created the Earth, and then the light and so on. He created the sun and stars a few days later. And she also said that it only LOOKS as if the stars are that old. But they aren't really old, only about 6,000 years. She said that we shouldn't believe what science tells us. If you have to choose between the Bible and science, you have to choose the Bible.

Within one minute, I had a reply.

From: Professor Jack Scott McNeil
To: Sam Billington
Subject: Automatic reply: 6,000 years

Thank you for your email. I am away at the Annual American Astronomical Society Meeting this week and am unable to read my emails. For urgent matters, please contact my secretary, Mrs Jill Whitehouse, email J.Whitehouse@ast.cam.ac.uk

Hmm. Great. You can always email me, Uncle Jack said. But now he's gone off, leaving me in the lurch.

THURSDAY

"After lunch we have another people-library slot," Mr Nolan said this morning.

"Instead of geography?!" Matteo called. "Yesss!"

"Who's coming today?" I asked.

"My dad," Christy said proudly.

"Your dad?" Luke said. "What does he know?"

Christy stuck out her tongue at him. "The Bible, Dumbo."

"I invited him," Mr Nolan said. "I thought, we've already had a university professor come in to talk to us about how everything came into being, and about how old the universe is."

"13.8 billion years," I said.

"And that turned out to be wrong, remember?" Tom said. "Your uncle didn't have a clue."

"And then Anna's mum came, and she told us that the universe is 6,000 years old." Mr Nolan put his arms in the air. "To be honest, I really don't know who's right."

"My mum, of course," Anna said.

"And so I thought we'd better invite Christy's dad. I mean, that's the whole point of the people library. So we can listen to people who are very knowledgeable. OK, get your packed lunches, everyone. It's time for lunch."

After our lunch break, Christy's dad was at the front of the class. He's quite tall, and big. My dad is the same (he loves cheese, and sausages, and he always needs to sample nuts after roasting them). But I think if there was a dive-bombing competition at the swimming pool, Christy's dad would win. And I don't think there would be any water left in the pool, either.

"Hello everyone!" he shouted with a big wave.

"Hello Rev!" we called back, and we waved, too.

"Hello Reverend Richard!"

"Please may I sit next to you, Rev Rich?" Esther asked.

"Reverend Richard," Mr Nolan said, "I decided to call you into our school because we have a bit of a problem."

"Oh dear. I hope you haven't got a blocked toilet," Christy's dad said. He looked a bit worried. "Or a maths problem. I'm not very good at maths."

"Don't worry," Mr Nolan said. "This is a problem just for you."

He stood up, switched the whiteboard on and wrote the problem on it.

THE BIBLE: God made everything
SCIENCE: Everything originated from
         a Big Bang

Christy's dad looked at the whiteboard. "So what exactly is the problem?" he asked.

"That IS the problem!" Mr Nolan exclaimed. "Surely those two statements cannot *both* be true."

Christy's dad scratched his shiny brown bald head. He looked surprised. "Why not?"

"Duhhh!" Luke called out. "If the Big Bang is real, the Bible can't be true, right?"

"I know a lot about the Bible," Christy's dad said. "But I don't know much about physics and astronomy. I read in the Bible that God made the universe with all its stars, and the Earth as well. I read that God still looks after the Earth. I read that he loves us very much – he even loved us before he made all of this. But the Bible doesn't tell us *when* he made everything. And the Bible doesn't tell us *how* exactly, either. So I can't give you the answer, because I'm a vicar and it doesn't bode well when vicars behave as if they're experts on everything."

Instead, Rev Rich told us about a man 500 years ago, who discovered lots of very interesting things about the universe, but he got into trouble because the church didn't approve of his ideas. The man's name was Galileo.

MR GAGA AND THE FORBIDDEN DISCOVERY

Today we've got Lady Gaga, but nearly 500 years ago lived a man whom we might call Mr Gaga: GAlileo GAlilei.

- *His dad wanted him to become a doctor. But Galileo preferred astronomy. And maths and physics.*
- *He invented lots of things, including a thermometer and a very useful mathematical compass. The telescope had already been invented, but Galileo improved it greatly. With his telescope he discovered new things about the universe.*
- *In those days, nearly everyone believed that the Earth was the centre of the universe and that the sun circled around the Earth.*
- *Galileo discovered something very peculiar. He discovered that Jupiter has small moons rotating around it. He thought: if this is the case, then perhaps the Earth rotates around the sun, and other planets might do the same! "Wow! God is helping me to discover all these exciting things - how cool is that?" he wrote.*
- *But the church establishment wasn't very happy: "What you say doesn't correspond with the Bible!" the Pope said.*
- *"Really?" Galileo replied. "But all I'm doing is showing you what a genius our Creator God is!"*
- *"Nonsense. Your message clashes with the Bible, so you aren't allowed to talk about it any longer. From now on, you're under house arrest!"*

Right. Well. IN A WAY, you can understand WHY the Pope was angry, as Galileo had in fact insulted him. In his book there was a man who looked very much like the Pope, and Galileo had called him "Simplicio", which is a bit like calling him "Idiot". Oh well...

Only about twenty years ago, just before the year 2000, the Pope said: "Galileo was right. We should never have condemned him."

JUMBLED WORDS

Galileo had a cool and clever way of writing things down. He shuffled letters to <u>make</u> a new sentence.

Have you heard of an anagram? It's a jumbled word or phrase. You just keep shuffling the letters until you get a new word or phrase. The following anagrams are things you can eat (answers at the bottom of the page):

- Smoothed, as pâté[1]
- Fin dish, chaps[2]
- Carb eaters flakes[3]

It's fun to hide food in an anagram. Anagrams can also be really useful for hiding secrets. Say, for instance, I really like Christy, but I don't want anyone to know about it. I can write in my diary "Yell! Tear risky chili". Or "chilly year is kilter". Or even "Kill rare chesty lie". You see? And nobody will ever find out!

With the aid of his telescope, Galileo discovered things that nobody in the world knew anything about. For example; Saturn had two spots (even with his telescope Galileo couldn't make out that they were actually part of a ring) and Venus looked a bit like the moon: you could only see the part that was lit up by the sun, as is the case with the moon.

When Galileo was alive there was no internet to upload your discoveries. Printing a book was very expensive. What do you think people did when they'd discovered something special? They sent a letter to a famous scientist. But you had to be extremely careful! What if this scientist read your letter and then claimed that he had made the discovery?

---

1 mashed potatoes
2 fish and chips
3 breakfast cereals

That's why Galileo hid his discoveries in anagrams. That way, he could always prove later on that it was he who had made the discovery.

Very clever! Some anagrams are practically impossible to work out. Try solving these two:
- *Harsh, bitter, wet heritage (clue: grab your umbrellas!)[4]*
- *We all rely on a boy often, no danger (clue: famous British sportsman)[5]*

"But what about the Big Bang?" Tom asked.

"I simply don't know," Rev Rich replied.

"Why are you here, then?" said Tom.

Florence jumped up, grabbed Tom's shoulders and shook him firmly. "Hey, behave yourself! He's the vicar. Show some respect, OK?"

Tom pushed Florence away. "Aren't I allowed to have my say?"

Florence stood up straight and gave him a stern look. "That was so rude of you. Just try to be a bit more polite!"

"Florence, sit down please," Mr Nolan said. "And as for you, Tom, that was very impolite. I think it's a brave thing to admit we don't have all the answers."

Anna raised her hand. "But it's very simple. The Bible says that God made everything in six days, so..."

"That's right," Rev Rich agreed. "The Bible does say that God made everything in six days. So it seems very simple. Six days are six days, right? But the Bible also says that God is a sun. Is God a sun?"

I shook my head. No way. He isn't.

"But it does say that! Look!" Rev Rich flicked through his Bible. "And look, here it says that God is a rock. Is God a rock?"

"No," Anna said. "But that just means that God is like a rock."

---

4 the Great British weather
5 Wayne Rooney, England footballer

"Yes," Archie chipped in. "He's strong. As strong as a rock."

"Aha!" Rev Rich said. "Do you know what you are doing right now? You hear or read: God is a sun. God is a rock. And you think: hmm, what does that mean? You don't think that God is made out of stone. Or that God is a star. No, you try to figure out what the author of the Bible means when he writes that."

"But God is the author of the Bible!" Anna said.

"I believe that God enabled *people* to write the Bible," Rev Rich said. "And those people did it in their own way. Using the language of their time. The people didn't know much about astronomy or gravity or what the Earth really looked like. That didn't matter. God explained the things that they needed to know in such a way that people would understand God's care for them. That he had made everything. That he loved them. If your mum was explaining something to a colleague at work, she would use different words than when explaining it to your two-year-old brother. She would kneel down and use language your little brother understands."

I tried to imagine how my mum would explain the difference between Cheddar and Double Gloucester cheese to my little brother, Snotty Simon.

The reverend went on to tell us that the Bible wasn't a physics manual with a step-by-step explanation of how you put a universe together. I would actually love a guide like that.

Suddenly there was a bleeping noise. Rev Rich grabbed his mobile phone and said, "I'm awfully sorry but I have to run! In half an hour I need to be at a wedding service."

"Dad!" Christy called out indignantly.

"Sorry, everyone. I would like to come back and talk a bit more to you all about this. In the meantime, here are two things for you to think about. Could I have a pen please, Mr Nolan?"

Mr Nolan gave him the whiteboard pen.

Rev Rich wrote two quotations on the board.

"It's a disgrace when Christians talk nonsense about the Earth, the heavens and nature and then claim that this stuff comes from the Bible. When they do this, non-Christians think that the Bible is full of nonsense. And then they won't believe anything in the Bible about Jesus or about God's new Earth either!" (Augustine, a 4th-century theologian)

"God has given us the ability to feel and a brain to think with. I can't imagine that we can't use both!" (Galileo, a 16th-century scientist)

With that, Christy's dad rushed out of the door.

SATURDAY

My mum and dad are ALWAYS working. Even when it's the holidays. And when we're snowed in or ill. It's because of the shop. They can't just close it, because then people will think: oh dear, the cheese shop is closed, we'd better go to the Megamarket, and then they go and buy their cheese there and think: hey, this is convenient, they also sell peanut butter here and bread and meat, so let's shop here from now on... And then WE would have to close down, sell the house and move out, onto the streets, begging for money and sleeping rough in cardboard boxes. You get the picture. That's why the shop can't ever be closed. There is only one exception, and that's Granny's birthday.

For this occasion, we even have a special sign which Dad puts up on the door:

DUE TO HAPPY FAMILY CIRCUMSTANCES, WE ARE CLOSED TODAY.

Dad deliberately put happy family circumstances on the sign. Otherwise people might think someone has died and they would say: "Oh dear, poor cheesemonger, let's leave him to mourn and go to the Megamarket instead – at least they are more cheerful there."

But I actually don't think celebrating Granny's birthday is a happy occasion. This is why:
• It's two hours in the car, each way!

- There are five aunties who each want to give me three kisses when we get there AND three kisses when we leave.
- One of the aunties has a hairy chin, very prickly!
- I reckon that Granny keeps her mouth open when kissing, as I always end up with a lump of spit on my cheek and I'm not allowed to wipe it off with my sleeve – that would be impolite.
- We're not allowed on the tablet or phone – we have to pretend we like chatting with our aunties.

The only good thing about going to Granny's today was that Uncle Jack was coming, too. It was worth the long drive there and back to see him. But it wasn't going to be easy. I had to sit in the very worst place in the car: in the middle. On one side was Snotty Simon, who was driving me around the bend by asking me, every time we saw a car:

"Woz dat Sam? Woz dat? Woz dat?"

"That is a car," I said.

"Is a car."

"Is a car."

"Is a car."

"A car."

"A CAR!"

"Is a space rocket. Happy now?"

Simon got really upset and started screaming: "No! Is a car! Mummy! Is a car!"

Mum turned around and said. "Yes, of course it's a car. Don't be silly, Sam."

"Tupid Sam. Is a car," Simon said, happily.

On the other side Lottie was poking me in the ribs because she said I was taking up too much room. "Muuuum! Sam is punching me."

"Stop it, Sam," Mum said.

"Mum! Sam is reading my book over my shoulder!"

"Don't do that, Sam."

"Mum! Sam's smelly feet are on my side!"

"Just leave your feet in the middle please, Sam."

"There's no room in the middle!" I exclaimed. "And why are you picking on me? Lottie can get away with whatever she wants!"

"What do you mean?" Mum said.

"She just called my feet 'stinky Stilton'!"

Mum sighed. "I'm sure your feet don't mind. They can cope with that."

I made myself as thin and invisible as possible and tried to use the rest of the journey to come up with ways to avoid my aunties' kisses.

"I am allergic to human saliva."

"I have a contagious illness. If you kiss me, you'll get an itchy, scabies-like rash all over your body."

"I've got a nasty cough. Do you know how dangerous it is to catch pneumonia at your age?"

"I've got more bacteria in my mouth than there are people on Earth."

A sign around my neck, saying "I only kiss frogs".

When greeting them, stretching out my hand as far as possible, keeping my arm stiff and leaning my head back.

I decided that the last option was potentially the most successful one, but when we finally got there I was ambushed by Auntie Janet, who grabbed me from behind, gave me three slobbery kisses, and firmly pinched my cheek. "Ha! My favourite nephew! Simon, isn't it? So good to see you again." Sigh.

I had forgotten to buy a present for Granny, so in the morning I'd quickly wrapped up a fossil and another special stone from my collection.

"I say," said Granny. "Stones. How very kind of you."

"Not just ordinary stones, Mum," Uncle Jack said. "Can you see what they are? Here, an imprint of a sea urchin. And this is a granite boulder. All the way from Scandinavia. From the last ice age."

"Well, well," Granny said.

"It travelled with the glaciers," Uncle Jack continued. "Look how nicely polished it is."

"Shall I look after them for a bit, Granny?" I offered.

"Yes, please," Granny said. "You take care of them. Imagine what would happen if I lost them."

Perfect. I got my treasured stones back.

We ate some birthday cake and drank lemonade (the aunties had cups of tea, millions of them) and after that we went to the boat Uncle Jack had arranged. It was called a Whisper boat, but I must say that none of the aunties made any effort to whisper. They chatted and laughed so loudly that all the otters and water birds fled – at least, I didn't see a single one.

But that didn't matter because I had the chance to talk with Uncle Jack. I told him about Louise and about the tornado flying through the rubbish dump, miraculously turning the junk into a Boeing 747. I told him that carbon dating of the Earth reveals that it isn't that old at all, and I was worried that this information would shock or embarrass him because he had believed in the Big Bang all this time.

But he was neither shocked nor embarrassed.

He had already thought about all these things. And that story about the carbon dating? It wasn't correct, he said.

MEASURING = KNOWING

You can use carbon 14 to accurately measure how old something is.

You need a special machine that counts exactly how many carbon 14 atoms are left. But this only works when objects are less than 40-50,000 years old. Older objects hardly have any carbon 14 atoms left. Therefore, there is much more interference in the measuring process. This leads to inaccurate results.

For instance, a bit of modern carbon could end up in your oil sample before you take it out of the ground, or even when you're putting the oil into your scientific measuring equipment. Or, sometimes, the machine that counts the carbon atoms gives off a false signal and you think you can observe carbon 14 atoms which aren't actually there.

Therefore, the values that are measured in coal and oil, which are much older than 50,000 years, are not correct. This is because the real carbon values are drowned out by "background noise".

If you want to know how old coal and oil are, you have to measure them in a different way, from the changes in different atoms such as uranium or potassium.

FIREWORKS!

A tornado that whizzes through a rubbish dump and accidentally creates a plane? That's impossible.

A Big Bang that causes billions of stars and planets to be formed? How is that possible?

You can compare the universe to a firework. Loaded with gunpowder, it is fired into the sky, where it explodes. All you can see is a beautiful cloud of colourful lights. It's a fantastic spectacle. But half a minute later, nothing is left... except for some leftover ash.

This is also how the universe started: all energy and space and time were packed together, and during the Big Bang everything was released! Everything exploded and dispersed. But after a very long time, thanks to gravity, pieces began to clump together and the first stars were formed.

Those stars won't exist for ever. Their mass is actually nuclear fuel, which makes them glow for a long time, but eventually burns up. If everything continues the way it works right now, in billions of years we will end up in a miserably cold universe. Without stars, without planets. There will just be some loose leftover pieces floating around.

PHIEEEEW... POP!

Without gravity, the universe would be extremely dull: everything would be constantly expanding and nothing much would happen. It's a bit like setting off a very cheap firework: you may hear a faint "pop", but you won't see anything.

But because of gravity, you get spectacular, loud, explosive fireworks. Stars and galaxies and planets are formed. Some stars explode dramatically at the end of their lives. The explosion makes them look like bright new stars (supernovas). Meteorites and comets are flying around and there are black holes, too. The universe is buzzing with activity!

HOW ARE STARS FORMED?

Stars are formed because of gravity. Gravity pulls huge numbers of atoms together. So many atoms are squashed together that they fuse inside the star and start giving off light.

RUBBISH

You have noticed yourself that:
- *Clutter just happens spontaneously.*
- *Constructing something or tidying up takes a lot of energy.*

Scientists have discovered that this applies everywhere and always. They call it the "second law of thermodynamics".

This law also applies in the universe. The universe may look very tidy, if you observe it from Earth. But if you take a closer look, you will find it is actually one big mess. In one place gravity is pulling specks of dust together, forming a star. But in another place, other specks of dust are creating even more chaos. And the newly formed stars are actually creating yet more chaos themselves, because of all the light that is racing through the universe in every possible direction.

"But we aren't descended from apes though, are we?" I asked, just to be sure.

Uncle Jack chuckled. "No, we aren't. Honestly."

I nodded. Of course I knew Uncle Jack wouldn't think that.

"No, but we do have the same ancestors as apes. That is something different."

"What?" I said. "So you do actually think..."

"Apes are more like very distant second cousins, that's what I mean."

SUNDAY

This morning over breakfast I told my parents, "Uncle Jack thinks that apes are our second cousins."

Dad nearly choked on his coffee. "Did he really say that?"

"Yes!" I said.

"You are so gullible, Sam!" said Lottie.

I stuck my tongue out at her. "He was dead serious, you know."

Mum shook her head. "Don't be silly. Jack was only joking."

"Or his brains have run wild," Dad said. "That IS possible. If you get too caught up in science, you could develop some strange ideas."

Later, when we came out of church, I WhatsApp'ed Uncle Jack.

Sam: Hi Uncle Jack, I thought the Whisper boat was epic but it was a shame we didn't see a single otter or rare bird

Jack: Hi Sam, yes, that was bad luck. There must have been quite a few around. Maybe Auntie Janet was just a bit too loud.

Sam: but I guess you were joking when you said apes are our second cousins

Jack: Strictly speaking we aren't second cousins. But if you were to go back many, many generations, some six million years in fact (so the mother of your mother of your mother of your mother... times half a million), then we would end up with the same mother!

Jack: So we have the same great-great-great-great-great-great-great-great-great-great-great-great-great-grandmother. So, we are kind of very, very, very distant relatives.

Sam: whaaaaaat?

Sam: so your granny was an ape?

Sam: with a tail

Sam: who swung around trees

Jack: Haha! You're turning it into a great story. But it is indeed true that we are very, very distant relatives.

Jack: Did you know that there are clues in your own body?

Sam: huh?

Jack: Your tail-bone, you know, the little bone at the bottom of your back-bone...

Sam: I fell on it once

Jack: That must have hurt! Your tail-bone holds several muscles together, especially in your bottom, and it enables your bones to move. It also protects your spine when you sit down, a bit like a car bumper. BUT compared to how it supported your ancestors' tails, your tail-bone isn't that useful for you.

Sam: really?

Sam: hang on

Sam: Mum says that is nonsense!

Jack: What? What is nonsense?

Sam: and that I mustn't believe everything you say

Sam: Mum says that God made Adam

Sam: (that's what the Bible says)

Jack: Yes! Did you know that "Adam" is the Hebrew word for "Man"?

Jack: God made mankind (and the rest, of course).

Sam: but you're saying we are just animals!!

Jack: Yes, that's right! Our cells, our DNA, our proteins: in that sense we are no different from animals.

Sam: huh?!

Sam: but we can think!!!

Jack: Correct.

Jack: I'll send you an email.

Jack: I'm not that fast with my index finger.

Sam: index finger??!! Haha! Do you use WhatsApp with your index finger?!

Sam: try typing with your thumbs, it's much faster

From: Professor Jack Scott McNeil
To: Sam Billington
Subject: Differences between humans and animals

Hi Sam,

You are absolutely right! We can do loads of things that animals are unable to do. We can think about all sorts of things:

- how to install a plumbing system,
- whether Granny Sue is being cared for well enough in her nursing home,
- what time it is in New York right now,
- whether the Earth revolves around the sun.

We can think about ourselves:
- how we are feeling right now, for example (happy? silly? sad?),
- whether we are in love,
- what other people think of us,
- whether or not we're brave enough to go to the dentist.

And there are other things people are good at. We have a language to express exactly what we mean to say. We can make clever tools. Wheels. Cars. Computers. We take good care of other people. For instance, people with a disability.

Some animals are also very clever. Crows, for instance, and dolphins. They have a pretty well-developed language they use to talk to each other.

And sometimes animals look after other animals that are drowning, injured or otherwise in danger...

Scan the code or visit: tinyurl.com/niceanimals

And there are animals that use tools. On YouTube you can watch videos about a sea otter using a sharp rock to crack open a shelf. Or a crow tossing nuts onto the road, waiting for cars to drive over them and crack them open.

Have you ever seen this film? A thirsty bird finds a way to make people give him a drink. Scan the code or see: tinyurl.com/thirstycrow

So animals can use language, look after each other, and work with tools. So how are people different? How are you different from a dolphin?

I think there is one very important difference:

You can think about yourself. About time. About why you are alive. About who has made everything. You can know God. THAT is what makes you special and unique. There isn't a single animal species that is religious!

I think God wanted people to come into being. People to share his love with. People who wanted to live in the world with him. I believe that God made this happen through an evolutionary process.

Best wishes,
Uncle Jack

MONDAY

"I have good news and bad news," Mr Nolan said this morning, after our daily Bible story. "Which do you want first?"

We all looked at each other.

"First the bad news," Archie said.

"All right then," Mr Nolan said. "Well. Hold on tight. Our school trip has been cancelled this year."

"What!?" Matteo shouted. He nearly fell off his chair. "Sir! You can't do that!"

"But we have the right to go on a school trip! It's the only fun day all year!" Anna said.

"School trip, school trip!" Luke and Tom shouted, and they began to clap their hands together in the air. Soon the rest of the class was joining in.

"SCHOOL TRIP! SCHOOL TRIP! SCHOOL TRIP! SCHOOL TRIP! SCHOOL TRIP! SCHOOL TRIP!!"

I decided to join in, even though I'm not that keen on school trips. Last year we went to Legoland, and I threw up in the rollercoaster, covering half the class with disgusting yellow gunk (on the coach I'd eaten four Coronation Chicken sandwiches).

The year before, it all went wrong on the waterslide. I was halfway down when I suddenly got stuck. When I looked up, I saw Tom and Luke blocking the water flow at the top of the slide. And then they launched themselves, speeding down like mad. Luke bashed into my face and I had to leave the swimming pool with a bleeding nose.

At the time, Luke said it was my own fault. "You were completely stuck on the slide, fat geek. You should be thankful. Without us, you'd still be stuck."

"SCHOOL TRIP! SCHOOL TRIP!!"

We shouted and clapped our hands together.

Mr Nolan ignored us and got an old, flowery Thermos out of

his bag and poured himself a cup of tea. He blew on it, took a sip and started doing some marking.

Luke and Tom carried on shouting, but Archie called out: "Shut your mouths or else!" and Christy and Esther whispered "Shhhh!" and "Be quiet!" and "Don't be such IDIOTS!" and at last it was silent.

Mr Nolan moved the essays to one side and looked up. "And now, the good news. We're going on a residential."

"A residential?" I said, shocked. I wouldn't exactly call that good news.

"Five days!" Mr Nolan said proudly.

Tom and Luke did a high-five. "Cool!"

"Epic!" Matteo said.

"We'll spend each night in a youth hostel and in the daytime we'll go to theme parks and the cinema," Luke added.

Matteo jumped up and knocked over his chair. "Disney World!"

"Alton Towers!" Rachid shouted.

"The zoo!"

"SeaWorld!"

"A tropical Aqua Park! With a spiral waterslide!"

"Well, that isn't exactly what we're going to do," Mr Nolan said. "We will be going on day trips during our residential, but with the aim of learning new things together. Educational trips."

"What?!" Luke was outraged.

"Sir!" Rachid moaned. He slipped off his chair onto the floor and lay there with his eyes shut.

"It's a joke, isn't it, Sir?" Matteo said. "Come on! Tell us it's a joke."

"Look here, boys," Mr Nolan said. "You all know that my favourite thing in the world is swirling around in a teacup in a theme park, just like you. But I've had a chat with Mr Fazeli and he said: 'Come on, Mr Nolan. It won't harm any of those children to actually learn a few things during their residential'."

Rachid stood up. He shook his head. "Poor excuse, Sir."

"Yes, Sir. In this class, you are the boss!" said Luke.

"And theme parks can be very educational, actually!" Matteo shouted.

"Yes," Tom said. "For example, you can learn that you shouldn't go on a rollercoaster after eating Coronation Chicken sandwiches!" Luke and Tom high-fived and laughed very loudly.

"What kind of things ARE we going to do then?" Christy asked.

"I'm so glad you asked," Mr Nolan replied. He typed something into his laptop and suddenly this loud, exciting, menacing violin music blasted out of the loudspeakers.[6] On the interactive whiteboard we saw a moon, a dark grey lump of stone, rotating in a large, black space. And then Mercury appeared, like a dried-out orange. And then a large, red planet with mysterious dark shadows.

"The red planet. Mars," I whispered, and I sat up.

The music got louder. There was Venus, enormous and yellow, and then, at last, the Earth – a blue ocean with large, green, drifting islands, and clouds floating above the surface.

Whoosh! The Earth moved to the background and Neptune appeared, spinning – much, much bigger than all the previous planets – and then Saturn and Jupiter came into view, followed by the sun, and the Earth kept getting smaller, until it was nothing more than a tiny speck, vanishing into the enormous space, with one star after another popping up. The stars got bigger and bigger, and then a giant red star appeared which was so massive, it didn't fit onto the whiteboard.

And then it went silent.

"Are we going to MARS?" Matteo shouted.

"Wahey!" Archie said. "We are going to Mars!"

"Yeah, right," I mumbled. "We'll go to Mars and we'll never come back."

---

6 Would you like to watch Mr Nolan's video clip?
Type in: tinyurl.com/biggerandbigger
or scan the code.

TRIP TO MARS

In 2025, you may be able to book a trip to Mars. But you'd have to think carefully about who and what to take with you. If you went to Mars, you'd probably NEVER be able to return to Earth! There simply wouldn't be room in a rocket to store enough fuel to get back again. So if you did go, you'd be stuck with the same, say forty or so, people for the rest of your life... in the same dome. A bit like sitting in the same classroom, but without break times and holidays, and you wouldn't be going home at three o'clock. If you fell out with someone and wanted to walk around the block to cool off, you'd have to put on your spacesuit first, because there wouldn't be enough oxygen in the air to breathe. And at minus 63 degrees Celsius, it would be pretty cold outside!

"Sorry, Archie," Mr Nolan said. "That would have been fantastic of course, and we did consider it, but it would be a little bit too expensive, a trip into space. No. But we are doing a science week."

"A what?" Luke said in disbelief.

"A science week." Mr Nolan rubbed his hands together. "This is going to be great, folks. We are going to do lots of research."

"And what exactly are we going to research?" Anna asked.

"The universe!" Mr Nolan said. "The planets. And the stars. And how God has created life. I mean, two weeks ago, a meteorite crashed through the roof of our bike shed, and Sam's uncle came and told us about meteorites and the universe."

Tom turned around and stared at me menacingly. "I don't believe it."

"Thanks, Sam!" Luke said. "Very kind of you to get this organized."

"Hang on!" Mr Nolan said. "This is NOT Sam's fault."

"OK, so it's my fault then," Anna whined. She tossed back her ponytail. "Because my mum was so desperate to come to school." She turned around to face the rest of the class. "That wasn't my idea, guys. SHE wanted to do it."

"It is nobody's fault!" Mr Nolan said. "All right, it is actually MY fault. Look, I'm just an ordinary teacher. I don't know anything about stars and planets and how old everything is. So I thought we'd invite a scientist. And then Anna's mum, Louise, came and we had some passionate discussions. We've also had the vicar. But he didn't know, either. I don't know if the Big Bang is true; maybe it isn't. Maybe God did make everything in one go, 6,000 years ago. He is perfectly capable of doing so. But on the other hand, God may have made everything through the Big Bang. I said to myself: how can we find out? So I was talking to Mr Fazeli about this and he said: 'Well, this is a school. The children are here to learn. Why don't you all go out and do your own research?'"

Mr Nolan banged the table with his hand. "So I thought: let's do it! Let's go and do our own research. Let's go and find out for ourselves."

"But what if we discover that once there really was a Big Bang?" Florence said. She sounded a bit worried.

"That would be great!" Mr Nolan said. "Because we would have discovered something new about the world that we didn't know before. About how God made everything."

"But Sir. If there was a Big Bang, then the Bible got it wrong!"

"Oh really?" Mr Nolan said.

He perched on the edge of his desk and got a banana out for a snack. "In the early days people believed that the sun rotated around the Earth. And they thought the Earth was flat and had four corners. They even thought that the Earth stood on stilts. Is the Bible inaccurate because it says the sun goes down? Or because it says the Earth has four corners?"

"It does look like the Earth is flat," Christy said. "And it looks just like the sun goes around. Because when you go to the seaside at sunset, you can watch the sun going down, further and further, until it seems to have sunk into the sea."

Mr Nolan peeled his banana. "And now that you know the Earth is round, does it make it harder to believe in God?"

Christy shrugged. "Of course not."

"It doesn't make any difference," I said.

Mr Nolan took a big bite out of his banana. "Do you know what I think?" he said, but it sounded more like, "Ooh you oh ot I ink?"

"Sir!" Anna shouted. "Don't talk with your mouth full!" She pulled a face.

"Oh, sorry."

Mr Nolan jumped off his desk and quickly swallowed his mouthful. "I know I shouldn't eat now, but I was really hungry. I only had a bowl of cereal for breakfast. But what I wanted to say is this: do you understand what I'm trying to say? If God made everything, then we're allowed to explore and find out more about it. About the stars. And the planets. And nature. And we don't have to be afraid of what we might find. We can only discover what God has really done. Isn't that amazing?"

"There's nothing amazing about it," Luke moaned. "I'd rather find out how the new rollercoaster works at Thorpe Park."

"Do we HAVE to come?" Tom asked. "Can I stay at home?"

"Look," Mr Nolan replied. "I can't force you to come."

Luke jumped up and high-fived Tom. "Yesss!"

"But if you don't come with us, you'll still need to come to school, of course, because it's not the holidays."

"No problem, Sir." Tom started to bang the desk with his fists in excitement. "Messing about."

"IT suite all day!"

"Two-hour break times."

"And in the afternoons, we'll have a new subject: 'football'."

"Sir!" Matteo shouted. "I would rather go to school as usual."

"Very well," Mr Nolan said. "I've arranged everything for you already. Whoever doesn't want to come will be in with Miss Smith's class."

"Miss Smith?" Tom cried out. He pulled an ugly face.

Miss Smith is the Year Two teacher. She smells of coffee and cigarettes, she has brown stains on her fingers, and she talks to us as if we are still babies in Reception.

"Don't worry," Mr Nolan said. "I will make sure there's plenty of work for you to do. And when you're finished, Miss Smith will have some extra tasks for you. She could do with a few more classroom assistants, she said."

Tom put his head in his hands. And Luke let out a massive sigh. "OK. In that case, we haven't got a choice. I'd rather go."

"That's sorted then," Mr Nolan said. "We will leave on Monday in two weeks' time and we'll be away for five days. I'll send out a letter today and you just need to ask your parents to sign the slip."

"Five days!" Martin said. "Um, Sir, what do we need to bring?"

"Clean underpants!" Matteo shouted.

Everyone laughed, but Mr Nolan said: "Very good, Matteo. We must definitely bring clean pants. What would we do without clean pants?" He picked up a pen and wrote on the whiteboard: clean underpants.

"Towels?" Christy asked. "Do we need to bring towels?"

Towels, Mr Nolan wrote. He rubbed his nose and squinted at the board. "And a sleeping bag. Please don't forget your sleeping bag."

Suddenly, everyone had suggestions about what to bring.

"Toffees, Sir! Write down toffees!"

"And sweets. But not cherry ones."

"Crisps."

"And a toothbrush!"

"Clean socks."

"Wellies."

"Notepads and pens."

"Sir!" I said. "Can I bring my telescope, please?"

"That's a good idea," Mr Nolan said. "Do bring your telescope."

"But I don't have a telescope," Archie whined.

"You can use mine," I said.

"Deodorant!" Florence said. "We must bring deodorant."

She looked around with a menacing look. "Especially the boys."

Why did she say that? I wondered.

Mr Nolan wrote on the whiteboard:

Clean underpants
Towels
Sleeping bag
Toffees/sweets/crisps
Toothbrush (and toothpaste)
Clean socks
Wellies
Notepads/pen
Telescope (if you've got one)
Mobile phone
Clean clothes
Warm jumper
Raincoat
Deodorant
  (especially the boys)
Shampoo

"Oh yes," Mr Nolan said. "And we will need a mum or dad to help look after you, so the trip doesn't go haywire." He wrote on the board:

Father or mother

"Or an uncle," I said. "Is that allowed?"

Mr Nolan turned around. "Of course! That's fine. As long as it's a trustworthy person – they'd need a certificate saying they can safely work with young people."

"So not a criminal, for instance," Luke said. He gave me a nasty stare.

"Maybe my mum could come," Florence said. "She plays the guitar. And she knows loads of songs! And she already works with young people."

Archie and I looked at each other. Oh no! Not Florence's mum.

Mr Nolan told us about all the things we were going to do. We were going to visit a "dark sky park", a planetarium with a cinema, and a museum all about natural history, to learn more about how life on Earth began. He said: "IF there really was a Big Bang, perhaps the theory of evolution could be true as well."

Anna shook her head so violently that her ponytail hit Christy's face. "No, that's impossible," she said. "The evolution theory is definitely not true."

"I don't believe that either," Esther said. "We really haven't evolved from monkeys."

"Only Sam, maybe," Tom sniggered, very softly, so Mr Nolan couldn't hear. He lifted his fist, so Luke could bump it.

"I don't think we've evolved from apes either," Mr Nolan said. "I think it's a far-fetched story, but we'll cross that bridge when we come to it. In the meantime, we can do some honest research though, can't we? Museums are always fun!"

"Do you know what FUN is, Sir?" Matteo said. "Rollercoasters!"

From: Sam Billington
To: Uncle Jack
Subject: Can you come????

Hi Uncle Jack,

We are going on a camp with school, to research if the Big Bang really happened and we need a mum or dad to come with us, but uncles are allowed, too.

Would you fancy coming???? You know so much about everything.

We are leaving in exactly two weeks.

Cheers,
Sam

From: Professor Jack Scott McNeil
To: Sam Billington
Subject: Re: Can you come????

Hi Sam,

How exciting, a residential. And what a good idea to do your own research and not just follow what other people believe and say!

I would love to come with you, but unfortunately I am very busy at the university. I have to give lectures and can't just get away for a whole week.

Can you postpone the trip until the summer?

Best wishes,
Uncle Jack

From: Sam Billington
To: Uncle Jack
Subject: Re: Can you come????

Oh.Too bad.

No. In the summer we break up for the holidays.

From: Professor Jack Scott McNeil
To: Sam Billington
Subject: Re: Can you come????

Hi Sam,

I understand why you're disappointed. I am, too. But remember,
you can always email me if you want to know anything!

From: Sam Billington
To: Uncle Jack
Subject: Question

I do have a question.

Did people come up with the theory of evolution because they
didn't want to believe in God?

From: Professor Jack Scott McNeil
To: Sam Billington
Subject: Re: Question

No, they didn't. The theory of evolution was discovered by
scientists who were researching how everything works in nature.
They found out that evolution happens in nature. They discovered
that life has developed very gradually. The more research they did,
the clearer this became.

Some scientists say: if nature came into being through evolution,
then that means that God doesn't exist. But they are wrong about
that. Evolution is about how nature develops. Not about whether
God exists.

Best wishes,
Uncle Jack

TUESDAY

We had circle time and had to say good morning to the next person on the register. We do this every morning, and Mr Nolan ticks our names on the list if we are there.

"A fabulous good morning, Tom!" Luke said.

"Good morning, Christy," Tom said.

"Good morning, Archie," Christy said.

"Bonjour, Florence," Archie said (you're allowed to say good morning in your own language, and Archie's dad lives in France).

"Good morning, Matteo," Florence said. "Mr Nolan, Karen wants to come on our residential. She will bring her guitar, she said."

"Karen?" Mr Nolan said.

"My mum! You know who my mum is, don't you, Sir!"

Mr Nolan tapped himself on the head. "Whoops. Of course I know who your mum is! It's fantastic that she wants to come. Now I can stop worrying about that bit. All sorted."

Matteo waved his hands in the air. "Hey! I still need to say good morning! Good morning, Mehmet. Sir. I have a brilliant idea."

Mr Nolan put the register away. "Go on then, Matteo, I'll do this later. What's your brilliant idea today?"

"At the Hancock Museum of Natural History, where we're going, I once went there and you know, you can go in for free if you bring a dead animal."

Mr Nolan's eyes grew big. "A dead animal?"

"A dead bird, or something. If you bring that along, they give you a free entrance ticket. And we can use the money we save to buy chips."

"Cool!" Luke said. He stood up. "Come on guys, let's kill some birds!"

Christy took a deep breath. "Don't be ridiculous."

"Hang on," Mr Nolan said. He put his hand up. "Matteo, so you reckon we can go in for free if we bring a dead animal into the museum? But why?"

"Because they stuff it for their collection!" Matteo said. "I've seen it myself! There is a room where they take everything out of the birds – the blood, and bones, drumsticks and all..."

"Drumsticks?" Mr Nolan asked.

"Oh well, whatever. I don't know what they're called. They're inside a bird, and they look like drumsticks."

"They probably call it a bird's drumstick," I said.

"So they take them out and the eyes too, and they put them on a plate, and stuff them with cotton wool and stitch the bird back together again so it looks quite real," Matteo continued. "There was a sign that said you got free entry if you brought a dead animal, I think."

There was silence for a moment.

"Do mosquitoes count, too?" Rachid asked. "Or flies?"

"I don't think so," Matteo said, and he wobbled back and forth on his special wobble cushion. "I think they have plenty of those."

"And you can't stuff them, anyway," Archie said. "They're far too small."

"Once we ran into a deer on the road with our car," Martin said.

"And then what happened?" I asked.

"We phoned the animal shelter," replied Martin. "They came. But it had died by then. They still took it, though."

"Shame," Matteo said. "You should have taken it home yourself. Then you definitely would've got a free ticket."

"At least five tickets!" Luke said. "A deer is huge."

"Hey," Archie suddenly shouted. "I know! I've got dead mice! Loads of them! In the freezer!"

Some of the class shouted "Eeeeek!" and "Yikes!" and "Yuck!"

"You've got dead mice in your freezer?!" Tom cried out. "Why?"

"For Alan," Archie said. "He loves mice. I defrost them first, of course. I put them in the microwave until they're lukewarm. And then I feed him."

99

"Who is Alan?" Christy said.

"My corn snake. He loves mice. A lot!"

Mr Nolan scratched his head. "I don't think you'll get free tickets if you bring lots of dead mice. I really think they mean wild animals. I mean, animals you find in the wild. I don't know if this will really work out."

"We still have nearly two weeks," I said. "That's quite a long time. If we all start collecting dead animals..."

"They will begin to smell, you know," Anna said. "Dead animals."

"They can go in my freezer," Archie said.

"Sure, and then you'll feed them to Alvin!" Christy said.

"Course not! And by the way, he's called Alan."

"My gran has turkeys," Anna said. "For Christmas. At least seventeen of them. Shall I ask her if she would kill one early, for us?"

"Nonono," Mr Nolan said. "We are not killing any animals for our school trip. I strongly oppose it."

"We can ask if other people have any dead animals," Archie said. "Canaries, maybe. Or a rabbit."

"Or if a pigeon flies into a window and kills itself," I said. That had happened to us not that long ago. Too bad we buried it in the back garden. That dead pigeon would have been worth a free entry ticket. Definitely.

"Or if your cat has died," Archie said. "Or your dog."

Anna began to whimper because her cat had just died (hit by a car). Christy put her arms around Anna's shoulder and gave Archie an angry look.

"We can put up a note at the corner shop," I said. "In case people have dead animals."

"Well it would save us a lot of money," Mr Nolan pondered. "And that would come in very handy. We could indeed buy chips with the money we save, for instance. So, IF you find a dead bird along the roadside..."

"We will bring it into school," I promised.

"And I'll stick it in the freezer," Mr Nolan said. "We never use the freezer compartment in the school kitchen anyway."

"But if the bird is not quite dead yet, we'll need to rescue it," Christy said.

Archie and I looked at each other. "Reviving a bird with the kiss of life..." Archie murmured.

"A straw!" I whispered. "We must always have a straw on us."

"If you find a bird that's still alive," Mr Nolan said, "you have to call the animal shelter."

After school, we pinned up notes at the local corner shops.

Do you have a dead animal?

If you bury it, it won't be any good to you anymore.
Instead, you can do a good deed and give it to us.
It will be stuffed and then you can visit your dead animal
at the Hancock Museum of Natural History.

Call in case of a dead animal:

Sam or Archie

Sam 07700 900912   *Archie 07700 900337*

Afterwards, we hurried off to my house to wait for the first call. But nothing happened.

Just before tea the phone rang.

"Yes, hello?"

The voice of an elderly man. "We've got a dead gull in t' gard'n. Could you come and get rid of 'im?

"Yes, of course," I said.

"Where are you going?" asked Mum.

"Just collecting something for school," I said, and I ran out of the door, jumped onto my bike, and cycled to Churchill Lane. The gull looked pretty disgusting, with feathers sticking out in all directions and blood and things like worms coming out of its stomach (I think they were intestines), and it smelled horrible. But still. It was worth some cash.

So I held my nose, picked the gull up by its wing and put it in a carrier bag.

"What have you collected?" Mum asked when I arrived home. The table was set and I could smell Brussels sprouts and sausages. I really don't like sprouts, but it did help to get rid of the smell of the gull.

"Oh, nothing," I said. "Can I just put something in the freezer?"

Mum looked into the carrier bag and yelled hysterically. "What is THIS? It's REVOLTING!"

"It's nothing. Just a little dead bird."

"Out!" she cried. "Throw it in the compost bin! No! Wait! Not in the compost bin! Throw it somewhere in a ditch!"

"Mum! This bird is worth money!"

"I don't care! Get rid of it! Take it out of my house, now!"

Dad came into the room and asked what had happened. I explained and he said: "Oh, but if you need dead animals, I can help you. This week I've already caught five mice."

"What?" I looked around. "Where are they?"

"Not here," Dad replied. "In the shop."

"Real wild mice? Have you kept them?" I asked, eagerly.

"No. I got rid of them. But if I catch more mice, I'll save them for you."

"Absolutely not," Mum said crossly. "No mice in my freezer!"

"But Mum!"

Mum pretended she couldn't hear me. She picked up the dish with sprouts and boiled potatoes, slammed it onto the kitchen surface and started to mash it all up. Large damp clouds steamed into her face.

Dad looked into the carrier bag. "I don't think this one will be of any value," he said.

"But they'll stitch it back together again nicely," I said. "They don't need the insides."

"Sorry, Sam. He's too far gone. Do you mind if we get rid of it?"

I thought for a moment. "You can have him if you give me two mice."

Dad smiled. "OK. Two mice in exchange for a bird. Can you hear us, Lydia! A born negotiator. You drive a hard bargain, my boy! You should go into business."

From: Sam Billington
To: Uncle Jack
Subject: Coincidence

But if there was a Big Bang, doesn't that mean that everything came into being by coincidence?

The universe and the world?
Does God actually still exist?

From: Professor Jack Scott McNeil
To: Sam Billington
Subject: Re: Coincidence

Hi Sam,

No, I don't think that everything came into being by coincidence. I believe in a God who planned creation.

1. Science can't say anything about whether it was a "coincidence" or "planned". Science describes:

- how a speck of dust floats through the air
- how a star comes into being
- how a plant grows
- how gravity works

But science is not about God and whether or not he masterminded everything.

2. Does God exist?

Science doesn't help me to prove that God exists.
Nor can I use science to prove that God doesn't exist.

3. Pointers

In the world around me I can see lots of things that point towards God.

The laws of nature, for instance.

I think it's quite logical to believe that there's a law giver, a God who made nature and all its laws.

The universe operates in a very precise manner.

It's as if it's been very carefully put together to make life on Earth possible.

Imagine that the force of gravity had been a teeny-weeny bit stronger...
Then the universe would have imploded again just after the Big Bang. POP.

Imagine that gravity had been a teeny-weeny bit weaker...
The universe would have expanded too much and stars wouldn't have formed. And Earth would never have come into being.

Do you remember us playing darts in the holidays? And do you remember how difficult it was to hit the bullseye with your little missile? Imagine that the dartboard was ten times further away. And you had to hit the bullseye blindfolded. And you only had one chance.

The likelihood of the universe coming into being by coincidence is like someone throwing a missile towards a gigantic dartboard blindfolded – and the dartboard is as big as the universe (that is 14 billion light years wide!).

And having to throw that one little missile EXACTLY into the bullseye.

Pure coincidence? This is such a coincidence that it can't be coincidence.

I believe that our God has created the universe deliberately, so that we can live on this Earth.

Best wishes,
Uncle Jack

YOU ARE AN ALIEN FROM OUTER SPACE

Have you ever heard of carbon? You can find carbon in coal. And in diamonds. But you can also find it in your own body. Carbon is one of the most important building blocks of your body. Just like oxygen.

The carbon atoms in your body aren't new. In fact, they are very, very old. Much, much older than you. Billions of years old. Once they were formed inside a star. Isn't that epic? The atoms that are part of your body were formed in outer space. You are made of stardust.

It's extremely hot inside a star. So hot and dense that a very long time ago three different types of atoms fused. Together they formed a carbon atom. Just the kind of atom that was necessary to make it possible for life to be formed. For you to be formed.

That is indeed very much a coincidence. It is in fact too much of a coincidence. It looks just like a highly intelligent being has been at work here! This is what a famous astronomer called Sir Fred Hoyle concluded.

THURSDAY

Our dead-animal-collection initiative is going very well. We've already got five mice and a budgie.

The budgie was Rachid's. "He was trapped in his bamboo stem," Rachid explained, waving round the plastic sandwich bag with his dead budgie in. "We think he fell head first, got stuck and couldn't get out again."

Anna buried her face in her hands. "That is soooo sad!"

"Maybe he had a heart attack," I said, to comfort her. "Otherwise he wouldn't have fallen like that. A bird doesn't just fall over."

"Did his beak get stuck?" Archie asked. "Upside down, right at the bottom of the stem?"

Rachid stook his head. "No, it didn't. Sir, where do I take him?"

"Just take him to the kitchen," Mr Nolan said. "And put him in the top compartment of the fridge. The freezer bit."

"My grandpa has a stuffed crocodile!" Mehmet suddenly said. "Maybe I can bring him in!"

"A stuffed crocodile?" Archie said. "That's illegal, you know! All crocodile species are protected!"

"Otherwise he would've eaten my grandpa. It was either my grandpa or the crocodile."

"Wow!" Matteo shouted. "Epic! How big is he?"

Mehmet spread out his arms a little. "About this big."

Martin shook his head. "He would never have managed to eat your grandpa!"

"No," Rachid said. "Your grandpa wouldn't have fitted inside that crocodile. Only if he was a baby."

Mehmet leaned back on his chair. "He's got very sharp teeth, you know! He could've easily bitten off my grandpa's hand and he would've bled to death. There you go."

"Maybe it would be better not to bring the crocodile along after all," Mr Nolan said. "Just to be on the safe side."

"How did you get all those mice?" Christy asked me in break time.

I thought for a moment. "That's a secret," I said. "My dad has told me not to tell."

Dad is worried that no one will buy cheese in our shop if they know we get the occasional mouse – as if he could help it! Mice are just very clever. Also Mum always cuts off the bits where the mice have been nibbling.

"Oh, so they've come from your cheese shop," Christy said.

I blinked. "How did you know – Wait. No. I can't say anything."

Christy smiled. "I won't tell anyone, you know that."

WEDNESDAY

Two extra mice and five moles.

Thanks to Esther's uncle.

He catches moles for a job. All day long he walks around famers' fields and other grounds, checking his traps. Moles are hard to catch, but his traps work well.

Anna thought it was dreadful. But Esther said that moles caused a lot of trouble.

"Because they dig up fields, church yards, sports fields, golf courses," Matteo said. "And your garden."

"They're horrible because they messed up my brother's football pitch," Esther said. "And he couldn't play for weeks. He was horrid and grumpy until they sorted it."

THURSDAY

A mouse and three baby rabbits.

The mouse was caught in our shop (but of course I didn't tell anyone) and the rabbits came from Archie. Well, they came from his mother-rabbit. "I found them in the cage, dead," he said. "Their mum forgot to give them any milk."

"Why didn't you give them a bottle?" Florence said crossly.

"How could I know?" Archie said. "She only feeds them at night and she must have forgotten."

Florence shook her head. If she were a mother-rabbit, she'd never forget her baby rabbits.

"Yes, it's very sad," Mr Nolan said. "But there's nothing more we can do."

There was a knock on the door and a lady came in. She was wearing a headscarf, a pair of jeans, and red boots with very high heels.

"Auntie Adira!" Rachid shouted, and he turned round. "That's my aunt." He patted his chest. "She's MY aunt."

Auntie Adira greeted us. "Hello everyone!" she said. "I am Rachid's auntie. I have come for the people library."

"Wow!" Matteo said. He was nearly on the floor inspecting Auntie Adira's boots. "Can you walk in those?"

"Matteo and Sam," Mr Nolan said. "Please could you put the rabbits in the freezer compartment?"

Auntie Adira glanced round. "What?" she said.

"They were already dead," I said. I didn't want her to think that we killed them.

"Did you see that?" Matteo said as we walked to the kitchen. "Those boots! Wooaaah! I've never seen such high heels."

"They looked like pencils!" I said.

Matteo punched me in the ribs.

"Yeeeahh! That'd be handy! I'm going to invent that when I'm older! Pencil heels! For children. You would never get lost, because you could just follow the pencil trail all the way back home."

"I'd feel sorry for little kids, walking in high heels," I said.

"Not a problem. Those heels would wear down. And if you found them too high, you could sharpen them, couldn't you? Very useful for burglars, too. So you'd know exactly where they were."

Suddenly, the door opened right in front of us. Miss Smith walked in and stared at us with her dark, piercing eyes.

"What ARE you doing?" she asked sternly.

"We just had to take something to the kitchen," I said. "For our teacher."

Miss Smith raised her left eyebrow. "Really?"

"Really. It's true, Miss," Matteo said. He looked at Miss Smith with the biggest smile ever. A smile that makes you think he's the cutest child In the world.

"All right then!" Miss Smith said. "But keep quiet in the corridor."

"Yes, Miss," we said in chorus.

Miss Smith slipped back into her classroom and we ran towards the kitchen. I opened the door of the freezer compartment, or at least, I tried to, but it didn't work.

It felt like it was locked.

"Let me have a go," Matteo said and he pulled so hard that the door flew open and a plastic bag of frozen mice fell onto the floor. Unfortunately, the bag ripped open and the mice rolled all over the floor. We quickly gathered them up and put them back in the freezer and hurried back to our class.

There was Auntie Adira in her high heels in front of the whiteboard, holding up an egg.

"Are you a chef?" Matteo asked.

Auntie Adira laughed. "No. I'm not a chef."

"She's a teacher," Rachid said proudly. "At a secondary school.

She's a geography teacher. Aren't you, Auntie Adira?"

"Can I eat your egg?" Matteo said. "Because I REALLY love eggs."

Auntie Adira shook her head. "No. I need the egg to explain something to you."

"How it can stand up without falling over?" I asked.

"No, I am going to tell you something about—"

At that point, the door flew open and Miss Smith stormed in, with a furious look on her face. "Can someone PLEASE tell me what THIS is!" she bellowed. She was holding a dead mouse. Well, she was actually holding him by his tail, so he was swinging back and forth.

Mehmet put up his hand. "A mouse!"

"Did you catch him, Miss?" Matteo shouted. "Can we have him?"

Miss Smith walked towards him and lifted his chin up with her index finger. "You know PERFECTLY well that I haven't caught a mouse. It was YOU who put this mouse in the kitchen! You and that friend of yours, that..." She looked at me.

"Not true," I said, and Matteo said: "No way! He fell out of the freezer! Because the door—"

"WHAT were you after? Hey? Giving me a fright? Well, too bad for you. You can't frighten ME that easily!"

"Uhm, Miss Smith?" Mr Nolan said. He tapped Miss Smith on the shoulder. She turned around.

"WHAT!" she snapped.

Mr Nolan looked sheepish. "I do think there is a misunderstanding here. I'll have a word with you at break time..."

"Well then," Auntie Adira said. "Rachid told me that you had been finding out how the Earth was formed, and I thought maybe I could tell you a bit more about it." She took a spoon out of her bag and tapped the egg.

"Watch out!" Esther shouted, but it was too late. The egg cracked.

"Take a good look at this!" Auntie Adira said, and she showed us the egg. It was full of little cracks.

"This is what the Earth looks like."

"Like an egg," Luke said. He sniffed. "Sure."

"And of course there's a chick inside, too," Tom sniggered.

Mr Nolan snapped his fingers. Tom and Luke suddenly looked like model pupils again, as if they found it really interesting.

Auntie Adira told us that the Earth is just like a hardboiled egg, with the Earth's crust cracked into lots of small pieces. Underneath the crust you have the Earth's mantle (that would be the egg white) and in the middle of the Earth is the core (the egg yolk) where it is mega-mega-hot – 6,000 degrees Celsius.

And then suddenly she clapped her hands and said: "This is just the theory. Now let's apply it. Who's ever tried to dig a tunnel to the other side of the world?"

All the boys had tried at some point, and three of the girls, too. I had done it in Reception. In the sandpit. I remember that I got as far as the water pipes; or at least I thought so, because the sand was so wet.

"And was anyone here successful?" Auntie Adira asked.

Of course nobody had had any luck, because it's far too far away. The Earth's crust alone is over 40 kilometres deep. And after that you hit the Earth's mantle. It's so hot that your drill head would melt instantly. So you can't get any further.

She told us that a long time ago, all the continents were stuck together and that they had slowly ripped apart and had travelled all across the globe just like ice floes drifting across the sea, but more slowly.

DIGGING YOUR WAY TO THE OTHER SIDE OF THE WORLD

Digging to the other side of the world? That would take you a while.

It's more than 10,000 kilometres to the other side of the world: 12,742 kilometres to be precise. If you went by car it would take you thirteen days.

WHERE WOULD YOU END UP?

You can find out online! Go to www.antipodr.com, type in where you live, and it'll show you! If you started digging in London, for instance, you would end up somewhere near New Zealand.

To be precise it would be somewhere in the Southern Ocean, so make sure your tunnel doesn't fill up with water!

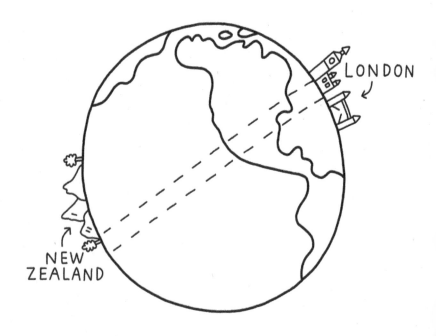

IMAGINE THERE WAS A TUNNEL TO THE OTHER SIDE OF THE WORLD AND YOU JUMPED INTO IT. WHAT WOULD HAPPEN TO YOU?

You would fall down, faster and faster.

If you were clever, you'd make sure there was no air in the tunnel, because if there wasn't you'd fall even faster. Once you were halfway, you'd be falling at a speed of 35,000 kilometres per hour! Wouldn't that be an exciting theme-park ride?

You'd race through the core of the Earth, without stopping, at top speed. But after you'd reached the centre of the Earth, you'd begin to slow down. And as soon as you got to the other side of the Earth you'd stop.

You'd need to get out quickly, otherwise you'd fall back down all the way to London...

HAS ANYONE EVER TRIED?

The deepest tunnel anyone has ever dug is the Kola Superdeep Borehole in Russia. It's just over 12 kilometres deep. That's pretty deep. If you walked down it, it would take you 2.5 hours. But you couldn't really get that far, as it's extremely hot, 12 kilometres down: 180 degrees Celsius!

In order to reach the centre of the Earth, you'd need to dig 1,000 times further than that!

That wouldn't work, because...
- It would get far too hot: nearly 6,000 degrees Celsius. Your tunnel would melt.
- The pressure of the earth above your head would be too great. Your tunnel would collapse.

CONTINENT JIGSAW

If you cut out Africa and South America and put them together, you'd find they fit together like two pieces of a jigsaw.

And, in fact, they <u>are</u> two pieces of a jigsaw.

All continents fit together like one big jigsaw puzzle. This isn't a coincidence, Mr Alfred Wegener explained in 1915. A long time ago, there was only one continent. A supercontinent: Pangea.

It ripped apart. So there were two continents: a northern and a southern continent. Gradually, more and more pieces started to break off and float around the world. This happened such a long time ago, we haven't got any photos or films to prove it. And yet we're pretty certain that this happened.

- The mountains along Africa's coastline fit exactly against the mountain ranges in South America. Even the geological layers are the same. It looks as if they were torn in half.
- Exactly the same fossils have been found on continents that were once linked together. Plants and animals from different continents are clearly related. It would have been impossible for them to swim across the oceans.
- In India, South America, Australia, and South Africa you can find traces of the same ice age. At some point these continents were all covered by the same thick white blanket of snow.

 Watch this video about the continental drift: tinyurl.com/historyofthecontinents or scan the code.

AS FAST AS A NAIL

- *Your nails grow between 2.5 and 5 centimetres per year.*
- *Your hair grows 15 centimetres per year.*
- *The continents move 3 to 15 centimetres per year. So somewhere in between the growth rate of nails and hair.*

At one point, India was where the South Pole is now. The continent slowly travelled towards Asia: 2,000 kilometres away. That must have taken a very long time, if it only moved 15 centimetres per year. That's right: it took 70 million years. Where India bumped into Asia, all the layers of sediment were pressed against each other and high mountains were formed: the Himalayas. If you go mountain climbing in the Himalayas, you can find fossils of seashells. Imagine this: that mountain slope was once an ocean floor!

"Was Britain also somewhere else?" I asked. "A long time ago?"

Auntie Adira nodded. "500 million years ago, Britain was near the South Pole! We moved north very slowly. And 300 million years ago Britain was near the equator."

Auntie Adira stretched out her arms and looked around. "Imagine that. Our country was a tropical rainforest, with loads of plants, and it was always hot. And it rained so much that we had lots of floods. If you dig deep enough, you'll find traces of that warm geological period."

"Palm trees?" Archie asked.

"No. Coal. And gas," Auntie Adira replied. "And 250 million years ago Britain was where the Sahara Desert is now. It was extremely hot. Britain was by the sea, then the sun caused that sea to evaporate. You can find the salt from that sea in our soil today – we mine it. The salt that was formed 250 million years ago is what you sprinkled onto your boiled egg for breakfast!"

"I never have eggs for breakfast," Matteo said. He sighed and looked at the egg on Mr Nolan's desk.

Anna raised her eyebrows. "So you also think that the Earth is extremely old?"

Auntie Adira nodded. "I don't just think that; I know it for sure."

Then there was a knock on the door. Anna's mum, Louise, peered into the classroom.

"Hello!" she said. "I'm here to collect Anna for her orthodontist appointment."

"Bad timing," Mr Nolan said. "Rachid's aunt is just telling us more about the Earth and Anna's just asked her a question."

"I can wait for a minute," said Anna's mum, and she picked up her bag and took a seat at the back of the classroom.

"Where were we?" Auntie Adira asked.

"We were talking about how old the Earth is and that no one really knows!" Anna said.

"Oh yes!" Auntie Adira said. "OK. If you see a tree, would you be able to find out how old it is?"

"If it's been cut down," I said. "You can see it. By looking at the tree rings."

"That's right!" said Auntie Adira, getting excited. "A tree gets a little bit fatter each year, when another layer is formed. And you can count the layers. You can see exactly how old the tree is. The Earth has layers, too. New layers are formed on top of old ones. And geologists use all sorts of techniques to measure the age of the layers. The deeper you dig, the further you go back in time. The top layers are the youngest and you can find mammals. The layers lower down are a lot older, and you'll find dinosaur bones, for instance. In the layers underneath that, you will find fish. And in the layers underneath those, you will find fossils of seashells. And of ammonites. These fossils look like snails, but were marine molluscs, called cephalopods. They were related to our octopus and squid! In the bottom layers you'll just find very primitive animals, which only have one cell."

At the back of the class someone coughed. "I don't want to interfere," said Anna's mum. "But..."

"No problem," said Auntie Adira. "Please go ahead!"

Anna's mum walked over to the front of the classroom. "I think the Earth isn't that old at all. Those layers could have formed in a very short period of time. I think they were formed during the floods, in the time of Noah. The entire Earth was flooded and that was of course a terrible disaster. At that point, the continents drifted apart in just a few months' time, and they collided so powerfully that the mountains were formed very quickly."

"Mum," Anna said. She was waiting next to the door, looking embarrassed. "Can we go now? Otherwise we'll be late."

Her mum looked at the clock above the whiteboard. "Yes, let's go! But let me just add one more thing – when the flood took place, coal and oil were formed, too. The forests were buried by a huge layer of clay and stone, which pressed so hard against the tree trunks and leaves that they very quickly transformed into coal. Or into oil, of course."

Auntie Adira shook her head. "Sorry, but I just have to—"

"In some places you can see a tree trunk trapped in coal, cutting across one or two layers," Anna's mum quickly added. "That shows that coal can't be as old as people say."

"But what about the fossils?" Archie said. "The fossils in the geological layers?"

"Those are the animals that got drowned during the flood!" Anna's mum replied. "Look, some animals like squid were quite slow, so they were swept away quite quickly. But the mammals ran up the slopes, so they can be found in the top layers."

"Muhum!" Anna shouted crossly from the corridor.

"I'm coming!" her mum said. "See you later!"

When the door had closed behind them, it was silent for a moment.

"OK," Auntie Adira said. "That was... uhmm... interesting. But that's not how I see it. Or what science has discovered."

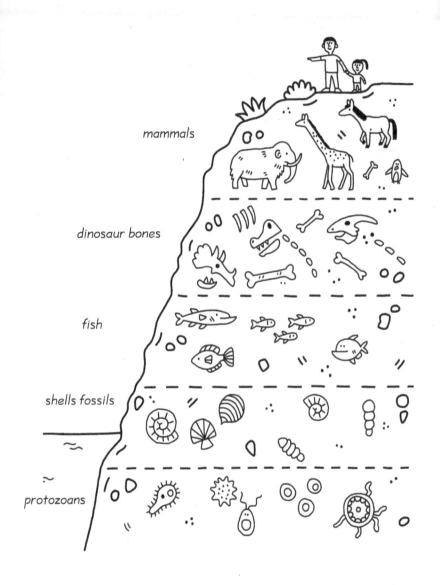

mammals

dinosaur bones

fish

shells fossils

protozoans

From: Sam Billington
To: Uncle Jack
Subject: The Earth only APPEARS to be old!

Hi Uncle,

Sorry for bothering you again, but could it be possible that the Earth only APPEARS to be old??? That the geological layers were formed really quickly because of the flood?

I have heard that they've found tree trunks poking through different layers of coal. This proves that coal was formed really quickly. Anna's mum says that this can only have happened through a global catastrophe (the flood).

Cheers,
Sam

From: Professor Jack Scott McNeil
To: Sam Billington
Subject: Re: The Earth only APPEARS to be old!

Hi Sam,

I know that story about the tree trunk sticking through various geological layers! Such stories are told over and over again, but if you take a closer look, it turns out that they aren't true. Or that there is a perfectly reasonable explanation, such as the shifting of geological layers.

I actually think your other question is much more interesting. You asked: could it be possible that the Earth only appears to be old?

I've got a question for you, too: do you believe what you see, or do you doubt it? If you see a carton of milk on the table, do you believe that there really is a carton of milk standing there? I'm sure you do!

It's different when you watch a magic show. You watch the magician saw a lady in half. Do you call 999 to report a crime?

No! Because you know you're being tricked. You know that the lady hasn't really been sawn in two.

Look at the Earth. There are so many signs that tell us the Earth is older than 6,000 years: geological layers, tree rings (there is even a tree that is nearly 12,000 years old), the layers of snow on the South Pole (which date back 700,000 years). You can measure this, and those measurements are very reliable.

Do you think you are being tricked? I don't think so. I believe that what we see is real: that the Earth is really very old.

Best wishes, Uncle Jack

From: Sam Billington
To: Uncle Jack
Subject: Re: The Earth only APPEARS to be old!

But wouldn't it be possible that God only created "ancestor species"?

So perhaps a fish and a beetle and a few birds and a wolf and a lion. And a sheep. And that all other animal species have descended from those???

From: Professor Jack Scott McNeil
To: Sam Billington
Subject: Re: The Earth only APPEARS to be old!

Hi Sam,

Of course that would be possible. God can do anything. He can create the Earth in six days or through a 14-billion-year-long process of evolution or something in between.

We can explore how God made the world, and we have discovered that he has done it through a long process of evolution.

Best wishes,
Uncle Jack

MONDAY

"Have you had a shower?" Mum asked this morning when I walked down the stairs.

"Why?" I asked.

"You're about to go on your residential," came the reply.

"Uhmm... I know." Do we have to be extra clean to go on a residential? Mr Nolan hadn't said anything about this.

Mum stood right next to me and sniffed. "You're a bit smelly."

I lifted my elbow and smelled my armpit. "I don't smell anything."

"Just leave that boy alone," Dad said from behind the newspaper. "He will get dirty again anyway."

But Mum was unrelenting. "You need to have a shower, Sam."

I sighed, went upstairs, switched the shower on, wet my hair, dried it off, and sprayed my armpits with a vast amount of deodorant.

"You smell lovely again, darling," Mum said. "Don't you feel much cleaner?"

"Oh yes," I said, as I sat down and put my knife in the jar of peanut butter.

"Your hair looks like a toilet brush!" Lottie said.

See. That's why you shouldn't have a shower in the morning. But Mum quickly changed the subject.

"I've made your packed lunch. Bread rolls. Ten, is that enough? And how many cartons of juice would you like? I'll put them in the front pocket of your backpack. Dad and I will come and drop you off."

"No, no; no need to," I said quickly. "I'll just take my bike."

"You want to take your telescope, don't you?" Dad said. "Too bulky to cycle with. We'll take you."

"And we want to wave goodbye," Mum said.

"All right then," I sighed. "But I'll say goodbye at home."

"Why?" Mum frowned. "Don't you want to kiss me goodbye on

the playground? What's going on now?! I hope you're not feeling ashamed of your mum!"

Uhmm.

I was worried that I'd be the only one who got dropped off, but luckily that wasn't the case. The whole playground was FULL of dads and mums, and they were all talking to each other, so Mum and Dad weren't too obvious. The coach was already there, and Tom's dad and Luke's were throwing bags into the luggage compartment.

"Sam!" Archie called. He was dragging a huge blue cool box across the playground. "Give me a hand with this, will you?"

I ran over to him. "What's in it?"

He dropped the cool box and opened the lid. "Nothing. This is to put the dead animals in!"

I had completely forgotten. If we left without our frozen animals, we wouldn't be able to get into the museum! We both grabbed a handle and carried the cool box into the school, through the corridor, to the kitchen, and we took all the bags full of mice and moles out of the freezer, along with Rachid's budgie, which we'd put in a lunch box with the baby rabbits. We put everything in the cool box, dragged it back through the corridor, out of the school building, and across the playground to the coach.

It was very heavy, but Dad picked it up and lifted it into the luggage compartment. My dad is very strong. That's because of the cheeses.

Florence's mum, Karen, was chatting with the coach driver. She was wearing shorts and trainers that were so white, they would hurt your eyes just looking at them. They complemented her legs at least, which were also very white. She was holding a guitar.

"Five minutes until we leave!" Mr Nolan called. He cupped his hands around his mouth, just like a megaphone. "We are leaving in FIVE minutes!"

My mum put her arms around me before I could stop her. "Have a great time, darling!"

I quickly wriggled out of her arms. "OK. Bye."

Luckily, Dad only gave me a high-five. And then I picked up my rucksack and quickly climbed onto the coach behind Archie.

"We're going right to the back!" said Archie.

"Not allowed," said Tom. "We're here already." He spread out his arms.

"There's loads of space!" Archie said.

"OK," Tom said. "You can come. But not Sam."

"No more room," Luke said, as he put his legs onto the seats.

Archie took a deep breath. He looked at the back row of seats. He looked at me. And then he looked at the back row again.

"I don't mind," I said. "You go to the back, that's fine. I'd rather sit on my own. I have a book to read."

"Good idea," Tom said. "You go and read your book on your own. Stupid geek."

Archie drew back his fist and let fly. It hit Tom's nose full on.

"Ouch!" Tom screamed. Blood came pouring out of his nose and he gave Archie such a hard push that he bashed into me; I tried to take a step backwards, but tripped over a bag that had been left in the middle of the aisle, and we both fell onto the floor.

I tried to scramble to my feet, but Archie was on top of me and Luke was hitting him, and then Matteo came running towards us, and he shouted, "Waheey!" and he jumped on top of Luke as if all of us were in a rugby tackle.

"Sir!" Christy called. "Sir! They're fighting!"

Mr Nolan stormed onto the coach. "What? What is happening here? Matteo, get off. You sit here. Tom, press this handkerchief against your nose. Luke, why are you fighting?"

"He started it!" Luke shouted, and he pointed at Archie. "He hit Tom on the nose!"

"Because he was calling Sam names," Archie said indignantly.

"Not true!" Tom said. There was blood splattered across his shirt and trousers.

"It's true!" Christy shouted.

Tom's mum came onto the coach and asked: "What's going on? Tom! What happened? Who did that to you?"

"Me," Archie said. He rubbed his knuckles. "He was saying nasty things to Sam."

"He called him a stupid geek!" Christy added.

Tom's mum tightened her lips and shook her head. She sighed heavily. "Come with me."

"No," Tom said.

"You come with me, I said." Tom's mum pulled him by the arm, out of the coach, and I saw out of my window that she was very cross with him. She took his bag out of the hold and for a moment I was worried that she would take Tom back home. But she didn't. In the middle of the playground, which was full of dads and mums and teachers and ALL the children of the entire school, she made Tom put on a clean shirt AND a different pair of trousers.

Suddenly Tom didn't look that nasty and strong anymore.

I even started to feel sorry for him.

"Not a very nice start to our residential," Mr Nolan started, when Tom had returned to the coach wearing clean clothes, with just a trace of blood on his upper lip.

"No, Sir," we said. "We're sorry, Sir."

"I don't need to explain to you that name calling is wrong, do I?"

"No, Sir."

"And I don't think I need to explain that hitting and fighting isn't the right way to resolve an argument either, do I?"

"No, Sir."

"OK. Great," Mr Nolan said. Tom and Luke had to say sorry to me, and Archie and Matteo and I had to say sorry as well, so we ALL said sorry and then Matteo opened his rucksack and said: "Who'd like some crisps?"

So the five of us went to the back seat and there was plenty of room. Matteo pulled out another two big bags of crisps from his bag, one cheese and onion and one ready salted.

"Only SIXTY seconds!" Mr Nolan shouted. Karen came onto the coach.

We ripped the bags of crisps open.

"Hey, we want some too!" Mehmet shouted.

"Pass them round!" called Rachid.

"And we're off!" Mr Nolan shouted. The coach doors shut with a loud hiss, and everyone waved, except for us, 'cause we were eating crisps on the back seats. Tom was the only one who

wasn't eating. He sat there with his arms folded, staring angrily into space.

It was a really long drive on the coach, all the way to Northumberland. "Because there aren't too many people there," Mr Nolan explained, "it's nice and dark at night – really good for looking at stars. We can visit the International Dark Sky Park. And you know what? They've got a brand-new planet trail. And we're close to Hadrian's Wall..."

"A WALL," sighed Tom. "Seriously. This is SO exciting..."

"It's a Roman wall, really old, and 120 kilometres long! And there are standing stones nearby as well."

"Standing stones?" I called out. That sounded brilliant for my collection.

Luke dropped his head into his hands. "You're kidding. This is going to be the most amazing school trip we've ever done. Looking at STONES."

"Hang on," Mr Nolan said. "Not just any stones. They're huge, prehistoric standing stones, called the Foal and Mare. I'm sure you've all heard about them."

"Can we go horse riding?" Florence asked, excitedly.

Mr Nolan sighed.

HADRIAN'S WALL

The Romans were tough, adventurous, and very successful. They knew what they wanted. You only need to read Asterix and Obelix to know this, or watch Horrible Histories about the Rotten Romans.

One time, 2,000 years ago, the Roman emperor Hadrian hiked with his soldiers all the way up to the northern corner of his empire - the north of England. Hadrian told his soldiers to build a three-metre-high wall to defend the country against the Scots, also called Picts, just like in Asterix and Obelix. For the next six years, 15,000 tough Roman guys worked their socks off to build a huge long wall that marked the frontier.

What would you do if Hadrian had asked YOU to leave school and build a wall to protect England?

a)   Ask the doctor for a sick note, hand it to Hadrian and hide under your duvet.

b)   Go and knock down that wall - we don't like those Rotten Romans!

c)   Yeaaah! Any excuse to miss school. Let's get building.

The Romans got to work straight away. Six years of elbow grease + a serious work out = Hadrian's Wall.

As if that wasn't enough, as soon as any red-bearded Scot tried to scale the wall, the Roman soldiers got right on top of them. Swords! Shields! Arrows! Anything to keep them out of the Empire! The soldiers on the English side were fit as a fiddle, after all that building, so the Scots didn't get very far.

Believe it or not, the wall is still there today! It's 120 kilometres long and you can walk the whole length if you fancy a bit of a challenge. At least you wouldn't need to worry about any Rotten Romans aiming their arrows at your behind.

Mr Nolan cheerfully continued. "So! We're going to see the longest Roman wall in the UK and the largest standing stones in Northumberland. Wow. Great stuff." He patted his own chest. "Not bad, Mr Nolan! Not bad at all. So what do you say? Thank you for organizing this, Mr Nolan! We're learning so much from you. And did you say there was no entry fee? WOW."

Luke and Tom looked at each other and shook their heads. "Completely bonkers," Tom exclaimed.

But when we finally arrived in Northumberland, they ran off ahead of everyone else to clamber onto the standing stones. (I knew straight away that these stones weren't really suitable for my collection.) I had a quick look for bones around Hadrian's Wall, without any luck. Oh well.

"Why don't we have this on our playground, Sir!" said Tom.

"This is pretty cool!" Luke shouted.

MOVING STONES

The Foal and Mare may be the largest standing stones in Northumberland, but they're tiny compared to Stonehenge, in south-west England. Have you ever been? If not, you'd better persuade your family to take you straight away. They are the most mysterious and famous stones in the world! Each of the eighty heaviest stones weighs 40,000 kilos, the same as a massive humpback whale.

It's hard to believe, but the stones came all the way from Wales. Maybe glaciers carried them part of the way. But, believe it or not, people did their bit as well, and they may have dragged them the whole distance – nearly 300 kilometres! They probably used rollers, ropes, and sledges to get these mega-heavy stones all the way to the plains where Stonehenge was built. An epic achievement. At least there weren't any steep hills on the way... Phew.

HOW DO YOU LIFT A ROCK WEIGHING 40,000 KILOS WITHOUT A MODERN MACHINE?

- *Recruit Obelix*
- *Organize a competition to find the strongest man in Britain*
- *Use a lever*

SEESAW

If you were sitting on a seesaw opposite the heaviest person in Britain, you wouldn't move an inch. The heavy person would keep their side of the seesaw firmly pushed down, and you would be floundering helplessly high up in the air.

Unless the heaviest person in Britain moved towards the centre of the seesaw. Suddenly, you'd seem to be the same weight. And you would actually be able to move that person up into the sky.

This is called leverage.

Leverage is something you can use if you want to lift something incredibly heavy. A piano. A garden bench. Or a stone that weighs 40,000 kilos.

We all sat down on the boulders around the Foal and Mare and opened our packed lunches. When we'd finished, we played tag on the hillside and then we had to get back onto the coach to drive to our campsite, the Happy Horse.

I was a little bit nervous because:

- A campsite named the Happy Horse? That sounded as if there were horses running around there. I don't like horses. Once I stroked a horse and it tried to gobble up my arm.
- I've never been camping in my whole life because we actually hardly ever go on holiday. Mum and Dad's cheese shop is so popular in the summer, with tourists buying cheese and salami. So if we do go away, it's in February. I don't really have a clue how to do camping, and in particular, how to put up a tent. I was dead certain that Tom and Luke would be laughing at me if I couldn't do it. So last night I'd especially taken time to watch some videos about how to put up a tent. I soon found out that there are many types of tents. Some you just throw up into the air and they pitch themselves, but others you have to put up with poles and hammers and odd-looking long nails.

Luckily, it wasn't too bad at all.

- There were no horses on the Happy Horse campsite.
- We didn't have to pitch tents, because they were already there. And they were enormous. So big, there were even bunk beds inside, and Archie and I were sharing a bunk bed. We would take turns to sleep in the top bunk.

The campsite boss was called Tony. He had a fluffy beard and a very fat tummy, and he wore blue trousers and big boots that made him look just like a garden gnome. And he was very strict.

"Toilets and showers are in the barn," he told us. "Please keep them tidy, or you'll have to clean them yourself. We don't waste water in this place, so shower tokens are fifty pence. If you want to wash your hair you'll have to be quick as the warm water only comes out for two minutes and after that it gets cold. FREEZING COLD."

"I'm not taking a shower," Archie whispered.

"Me neither," I whispered back.

"The campsite has to remain TIDY at all times." Tony looked around. "Tidy up your mess and make sure you don't leave any food out. There's a pack of wolves that roams around in the woods and you wouldn't want to attract them."

Everyone started to chatter amongst themselves.

"What?"

"Wolves?"

"Where!"

"Here! Here, he said!"

"If that's true, I'm not sleeping in a tent," said Florence.

"OK. Can I PLEASE have your attention!" Tony called out.

Anna put up her hand and looked around to see if we were copying her.

Mr Nolan whistled with his fingers. "Let Tony finish, please."

"They won't harm you," said Tony when everyone had gone quiet. "Those wolves. Under normal circumstances they don't attack people."

Florence's mum frowned. "Under normal circumstances?"

"What if they're hungry?" asked Martin.

Tony shrugged. "They're likely to go for a rabbit. Or a bird."

Archie and I looked at each other. We were thinking the same thing: the cool box. The cool box with our frozen animals.

"Excuse me," I quietly asked. "Do you happen to have a freezer which we can use for some frozen... uhmm..."

"...meat," Archie quickly chipped in.

"...which we can use for some frozen meat?"

"No problem. There's a fridge in the barn with a freezer compartment."

"Maybe hold off for a minute," Mr Nolan said, and he followed Tony out of the tent.

I suddenly felt a poke in my ribs. It was Matteo's elbow. "Sam, you've got binoculars, haven't you?"

I shook my head. "A telescope."

"That's fine too. Let's go and put out a trail." Matteo grinned.

"A trail?"

"A trail of food," he said. "We've got to lure them, man. This is totally awesome. I've never seen a wolf in my life."

MONDAY NIGHT

Archie and I were on cooking duty this evening. There was a kitchen in the barn with pots and pans so big you could fry a small child in one (which of course we didn't). We had to throw in kidney beans, diced pepper, onion and minced meat. A bit like a chilli con carne without the chilli. Once it was bubbling and foaming, it was ready. It looked disgusting, but Mr Nolan said it was a perfectly adequate meal, and the most popular dish at school camps. All we had to do was drain it, he said.

"What's draining?" I asked.

"Let me show you," Mr Nolan said. He lifted the pan off the hob, tilted the lid slightly and held the pan at an angle so the liquid could run off into the sink. A few beans fell out and a huge cloud of steam escaped from under the lid.

"Ouch!" Mr Nolan screamed. And then with a loud clatter, the lid fell into the sink. And then the mush of mince, kidney beans, pepper and onion followed.

Florence came into the barn. "Sir, where are the— Sir! What are you doing?"

"Mr Nolan burned his hand," I shouted. I quickly turned on the cold tap. "Put your hand under the cold water, Sir!"

The water poured over Mr Nolan's fingers and into the chilli.

Florence wrinkled her nose. "Yikes. What is THAT? It looks like sick!"

"That's our dinner," Archie said. He picked up the skimmer and started to scoop the beans out of the sink.

"That WAS our dinner," Mr Nolan said. "Sorry, boys. I'm afraid we'll have to go to McDonald's tonight."

"No worries, Sir," I said, and patted Mr Nolan on the back. "No problem."

From: Sam Billington
To: Uncle Jack
Subject: Trick??

Hi Uncle,

I'm sending you this message from our school camp. I got a seat at the back of the coach and we saw standing stones.

Tonight we went to McDonald's because the kidney beans had fallen out of the saucepan (thanks to gravity).

We've got free time now until dark, and then we're going to the moors to watch the stars. I brought my telescope.

I've got a question. Do you think that Jesus walked on water? I once watched a trick on MythBusters where they walked on water, or at least, it looked like it, but in reality there was a plank underneath the surface.

And do you think he really came back to life? Because that is completely impossible.

And what about the parting of the Red Sea that allowed Moses and all the Israelites to walk on the bottom of the sea across to the other side?

Cheers,
Sam

From: Professor Jack Scott McNeil
To: Sam Billington
Subject: Re: Trick??

Dear Sam,

I hope you're having a great time on your school camp! Too bad you lost the kidney beans. I'm sure you were absolutely gutted that you had to go to McDonald's instead ;-)

You're actually asking me what I, as a scientist, think about the miracles in the Bible.

Let me first explain something about the laws of nature: by observing and measuring things, scientists have discovered that a lot of what happens in nature happens according to fixed patterns. We call these patterns the laws of nature. For example, according to the law of gravity, objects will always fall downwards. If you turn over a pan with kidney beans, the beans will fall out.

Does everything work according to the laws of nature, like gravity? Or could miracles happen, too?

I believe that God made physical laws so that everything works in the same way every time. That's a good thing, because otherwise it would be total chaos. But very occasionally, and for a good reason, God can decide to let nature take a different course. So, for example, I believe that God enabled Moses to part the water of the Red Sea (maybe because God brought along an extremely strong wind, just, as it happened, at the right moment). And I can believe that Jesus really did walk on water (even if that's impossible according to the law of gravity). And I believe that Jesus came back to life after he'd already been dead for three days (although the laws of nature wouldn't allow that).

But it is important to remember that these miracles always have a special meaning. They're not just random magic tricks. God uses them to teach us something important. For instance, because of Jesus' resurrection we know that God is stronger than death, and that gives us the hope that we can live on even after this life.

Uncle Jack

PS: When you do your stargazing tonight, you must look out for Saturn. You can see it from 10.30 p.m. in the south east.

After dinner we played games. Boys against girls. To see how many of us could stand together on one car tyre. The girls won. They managed with six of them. And then we played catch, with the girls catching the boys, and then when it was too dark Florence's mum, Karen, got her guitar out of the tent and said we'd sing a few songs. Camp songs.

"Camp songs?" said Archie.

"Yes, like Ten Green Bottles," said Florence's mum. "And the Banana Song. You know that one, don't you?"

Archie and I looked at each other and we shook our heads. We didn't know any of those songs! And we definitely didn't want to learn them, either.

"We could go stargazing," I said.

"Epic plan!" Archie said.

"But we'd have to go up onto the moors," I said. "We can't do it here, too many trees."

"I think singing songs is a better idea," said Florence's mum. "With those wolves roaming around."

"I have a suggestion," said Mr Nolan. "Those who'd like to go stargazing can come with me and Sam, and those who'd rather stay here and sing can stay with Karen."

"I'll go with you, Sir!" said Matteo.

"I'll stay here," Florence said.

"Me too," said Esther. "I'm definitely not leaving this place."

All the girls except Christy stayed with Florence's mum. As we walked towards the moors with our torches, we could hear them singing. Shake bananas, shake, shake bananas... Go bananas, go, go bananas...

"Hmmph," moaned Mehmet. "They've gone totally bananas."

And then we got to the moors.

I put up the telescope, pointed it to the south east, and focused it on Saturn. There it was.

"Wooooow!" said Christy, who was allowed to have a go after me. "I've never ever seen such an amazing planet."

"I know," I said. "It's my favourite planet. And can you see the rings? They're made out of ice."

"What?" shouted Matteo. "Like ice-cream? I want to see that. Totally awesome. Saturn is my favourite planet, too."

"Can I have a look?" said Tom. "Hey! Yes. I can see it!"

"Can we have a quick look at the moon, too?" asked Luke.

"We'll keep that for tomorrow," Mr Nolan said. He patted me on the back. "Thanks, Sam. That was really special."

"That was cool," I heard Tom say to Luke as we walked back in the dark. "For my birthday, I'm going to ask for a telescope as well."

At that moment, I felt like I was playing football and had just scored the winning goal.

TUESDAY

Today we went to the university.

A real university. I thought it would be an old building, with wandering professors in black gowns and black hats. But it was more like a really big school, and I couldn't see any professors, only normal people in shirts and trousers and some with white lab coats on. But we did go to a real lecture hall with tip-up seats and tables and Dr Owens did a mini lecture for us. Too bad she wasn't a professor, but she did know a lot and she looked fun, with long red hair.

"Who can tell me what the smallest part of your body is?" she asked.

Esther put up her hand. "Your appendix."

Matteo jumped up and waved his arms round. "Yes! My appendix has gone! It made me really ill. So I had to go to hospital and then they took it out. It was just in time, the doctor said. Otherwise it would've burst. But I made it."

"Phew," Dr Owens said. "But actually, your appendix is not your smallest body part."

Matteo sat down again, but because his seat had tipped up, he fell in between two seats, onto the floor. "Ouch!" he groaned. "My bottom! Sam. Help."

I put out my hand and pulled him up.

"What is even smaller than your appendix?" asked Dr Owens.

"Your eye!" said Anna.

"Smaller."

"Your teeth!" said Anna.

"Smaller." Dr Owens looked around the lecture room. I was thinking about my body parts.

"Your nail!" Archie shouted. "The one on your little toe!"

"Smaller."

Christy put her hand up. "A single eyelash?"

"Smaller."

"A blood cell?" I said.

Dr Owens threw up her arms in the air as if I had scored a goal. "Yes! Excellent! Your blood cells are VERY small."

"Stupid geek," said Tom.

Christy turned around. "Shut up, Tom."

"Yes, Tom," I said. "Shut up. I want to listen."

"And you don't only have blood cells," Dr Owens continued. "You have all sorts of cells. You are, in fact, a kind of Lego construction."

LEGO

Did you know that each human being is like a gigantic Lego construction?

You're made up entirely of small blocks which fit perfectly together. At one time – nine months before you were born, to be precise – you were just one cell.

But now you are 37 trillion cells. That is so many that even when you try to imagine it, your brain goes POP. But if you lined up all those cells in your body you'd have created a cord so long, it could go around the world eight times.

A CELL IS LIKE A SPACESHIP

A single cell is far too small to see with your naked eye. Let's blow up a single cell until it is 1 billion times its normal size. Now we can have a look inside.

We're entering a massive spaceship.
Wait a minute. Hey! Stop! We'd better get on a bike, because this spaceship is 20 kilometres long!
There are thousands of entrances. It doesn't matter which one you take.
Robots are at work all over the place. These robots are called proteins.

There are thousands of different robots, and they all have their own job to do within the spaceship. The robots do all sorts of things: they communicate with other robots, they maintain the spaceship, they manufacture new robots, and they transform chemical compounds into other compounds.

The spaceship is beautifully organized:
- There are train tracks going in all directions, so small carriages can be sent from one place to another.
- There are power stations which turn food into fuel.
- There are industrial zones where new robots are being manufactured and old robots dismantled.
- There is a waste-collection service.
- There's an enormous, spherical library (it takes fifteen minutes to walk right through it!) with all the information that could be needed for the running of the spaceship.
- There are special library robots, which constantly check this information. If there's a little error in one of the books, it'll be instantly corrected. By a different type of robot, of course.
- The outer wall of the spaceship is four metres thick! This provides good protection against enemies from space. There are special gates with sensors. These sensors can detect if visiting components should be allowed in, or not.

And imagine this: JUST as you enter the cell, it begins to split.

Within a single hour the spaceship has divided itself into two completely new spaceships. Both have a library with all the relevant information, a power station, new robots, waste collection services, and train carriages.

LITTLE CHAMBERS

Robert Hooke lived in the seventeenth century. He had a microscope, which he used to study all sorts of things. Cork, for instance. He cut small slices of cork and studied them with his microscope. "There are lots of little chambers in cork," he said to

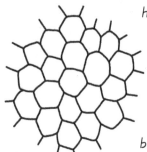

himself. "They look just like the hexagonal cells in a honeycomb. Or the bare cells in monasteries where monks live!" Hooke didn't have a camera, because they hadn't been invented yet. So he drew exactly what he saw. He had no idea what purpose the chambers served, but he called them "cells".

"You all started as one cell, a long time ago," Dr Owens said, and she showed us a clip on the whiteboard. "You didn't look like a human being then. Not even like a baby. In order to see yourself, you'd have had to look through a microscope – and you wouldn't have seen anything more than a small round ball. A cell. But a cell that was full of life! That single cell split into two cells. Those two cells split again. And those four again.

"And then something really special happened. Each cell received its own specific job. Four weeks after you were formed, cells were working together to form a heart. Other cells gathered together to create blood vessels. Or a backbone.

"How did those cells know what to do?" she asked.

"In each of your cells there is a kind of computer programme. It tells the cell what to do," Dr Owens continued. "Should it produce blood? Or should it join together with other cells to become a muscle? Should it be sending off signals in your brain? Should it become a "soldier cell" and join the fight against intruders?

"The cells work well together, and they know exactly what to do. Together they make sure you stay healthy and that you can walk and eat and think.

"That kind of computer programme in your cells is called deoxyribonucleic acid."

"This is SO interesting," yawned Tom. He sprawled on his chair and got out his mobile. "Don't worry about the name," Dr Owens said. "Just remember that we call it DNA." [7]

THE LANGUAGE OF GOD

What does DNA look like?

Like tiny strings. If you take a close look at these strings, you'll see they're actually like small rope ladders. Small rope ladders that twist around into a spiral staircase. If you wanted to climb up one of these rope ladders, it would take you quite a while. There are no less than 3 billion steps - and there's a rope ladder like this in every cell in your body!

Every step of the rope ladder has a special code. And the order of the steps determines
- *your type of hair*
- *the colour of your eyes*
- *which finger is longer: your index or your ring finger*
- *whether you look more like your dad or your mum*
- *whether you're naturally good at gymnastics*
- *whether you have a natural talent for music*

One of the scientists who led the enormous project of decoding the entire human DNA is Francis Collins. Francis was absolutely thrilled with his discovery. And he wasn't the only one. Bill Clinton, who was then President of the United States, said: "This is totally awesome! We have decoded the language of God!"[8]

"DNA?" I asked. "That's how they hunt down criminals, isn't it?"

"Exactly!" said Dr Owens. "Imagine that your teacher tried to burgle someone – let's call her Granny Johnson..."

---

7 Here's a fun video about cells, called the "Cell Rap": tinyurl.com/thecellrap and another about DNA: tinyurl.com/fundnarap

8 Francis Collins' book *The Language of God* is awesome and written very clearly – do read it when you are a bit older. You can learn a lot more about how you can take both science and the Bible seriously.

Mr Nolan looked up, taken aback. "What?"

"So that's what you do in your spare time, Sir!" Florence said.

"Yes, Sir!" said Matteo. "Just admit it!"

Everyone started to talk and laugh.

"Sir!"

"How could you!"

"Poor Granny Johnson!"

"All right. All right," Dr Owens quickly said. "Not your teacher. We all know he would never do such a thing. But imagine that someone else tried to break into Granny Johnson's."

"Miss Smith," I suggested.

"No, not Miss Smith," said Mr Nolan. "Let's say... uhmm..." Mr Nolan scratched his head. "Andy. Awful Andy."

Dr Owens nodded. "Okay. Imagine that Awful Andy burgles Granny Johnson. He has to take care not to leave any fingerprints, of course. Because everyone has a unique fingerprint. If the police find Andy's fingerprints, he'll be caught."

"Not if he wears gloves," said Archie.

"Exactly!" said Dr Owens. "That would be very clever. But Andy forgets one very important thing. He forgets to wear a hat. And that's where he goes wrong. For Andy accidentally loses a hair. These things happen. There are cells at the bottom of a single hair. And those cells contain Andy's DNA. He's found out!"

UNIQUE!

Every person has their own unique DNA. No one else in the world has the same DNA as you. Well, unless of course you have an identical twin. Because then you both started off as the same cell.

HOW LONG DOES A CELL LIVE?
- *a white blood cell: 2 days*
- *a skin cell: 30 days*
- *a red blood cell: 120 days*

- *a liver cell: 18 months*
- *a bone cell: 6 years*
- *a brain cell: an entire life*

R.I.P. – REST IN PEACE

Sadly, most cells are very short-lived. You lose nearly 50 million cells per minute. Dead skin cells fall onto the floor, and end up in your vacuum cleaner. Dead blood cells or liver cells are disposed of in a different way. They end up in the toilet. The sad thing for those cells is that they've worked so hard for you. And you hadn't even noticed they'd gone. In fact, they were instantly replaced by new cells.

"And now you're going to look at your own DNA," Dr Owens said. And she led us out of the lecture room, through the corridors to a real laboratory. There were shelves with test tubes and funnels and round bottles and glass dishes and pipettes; there were scales, taps, small hoses, burners, computers, and microscopes.

"This place is epic," I whispered.

"This is where I want to work when I'm older!" Archie said.

"But I thought you were going to work with snakes," I said.

"Yes, but I'm ALSO going to work in a lab. I'll take venom out of snakes. Just like Steve Backshall from Deadly 60 – he's done loads with venomous snakes."

There was a tray with small bottles of fizzy pop by the sink.

"Perfect!" cried Matteo. "I was feeling mega thirsty."

He'd almost finished his drink when Dr Owens explained what we were meant to do. We had to take a large sip of the drink without swallowing it. Instead, we had to swirl it around our mouth for two minutes, with great gusto, so the cells inside us could mix with the drink. Then we had to spit it out into a small cup and carefully pour the liquid into a test tube.

Most of our class really didn't like it.

"That's gross!"

"But it's full of spit!"

"Yikes, Sir. I've got it on my hand!"

"Now add a bit of washing-up liquid," said Dr Owens. "Until your test tube is half full. Then put the lid back on and gently jiggle the tube back and forth."

Matteo started to shake the tube violently as if he was shaking a bottle of squirting cream.

"Don't shake it!" cried Dr Owens. "Just gently rock it!"

Then we used a pipette to add a few drops of pineapple juice to our test tube. And then we carefully added a bit of freezing-cold alcohol. "And now you can put your test tube back on the rack, and wait for a minute. If you like, you can have the rest of your drink now.

"I didn't drink anything. Instead, I rested my chin on my hands and looked intently at my test tube. Very slowly something began to appear between the layer of alcohol and spit. Something white. A kind of small, transparent cloud.

"Hey!" said Matteo, who was also staring at his test tube. "That looks like the stuff my grandpa puts his false teeth in."

Anna nearly choked on her drink and Christy made a noise that sounded like vomiting.

"You're totally gross, Matt!" said Florence, and she hit Matteo with such force that he bashed against the table with the test tubes on.

"Watch out!" I shouted crossly. "You're ruining the experiment!"

"Now let's take a cocktail stick, and put it in the test tube, and stir it round very carefully," Dr Owens said.

I did exactly as she told us to, and the small white cloud twisted itself round my cocktail stick. I managed to lift it out of the test tube.

"Look!" said Dr Owens. "That's your DNA!"

"Wooooow," I whispered. "Look at that." There was my DNA! On a cocktail stick! Luke and Tom compared their sticks.

"That's gross! Look at mine!"

"Mine looks like egg white!"

Matteo put his hand up. "Is it edible?"

"I wouldn't try," replied Dr Owens. "I think it'll taste like washing-up liquid."

"Plus, you're not allowed to have alcohol yet," Mr Nolan said.

Very carefully, I put my DNA back in the test tube and put the lid on. I decided to take it home with me. A fabulous addition to my collection. I'd ask Mum if I could have a glass cabinet. That way I could put my fossils and shark teeth on display, as well as the test tube with my very own DNA.

And anyone who wants to see it will need to pay.

"Tonight we're watching a film about DNA," Mr Nolan said that evening, after we got back to the campsite and had finished eating our chicken drumsticks.

"Oh no," said Luke.

"You must be kidding," said Tom.

"Oh, come on, Sir!" Mehmet called. "You're cruel, you know."

"We've been working hard all day," said Florence. "Can't we

have a break from that stupid DNA?"

"It's awesome stuff," Mr Nolan said. He clapped his hands together. "Come on. We're going to the barn."

We all went to the large barn, where there was a projector and a screen.

"I have to warn you," Mr Nolan said. "This isn't a film for wimps."

Tom and Luke laughed.

But during the film I heard them scream more than once.

It was actually quite scary. It was about two children who went along with their granddad to an island where dinosaurs had been bred from blood, and the dinosaurs were massive and wild, and they broke free and chased people and one man was actually eaten alive.

"Is that really possible?" Christy asked afterwards. "Is it really possible, breeding dinosaurs?"

"I'll ask my uncle," I said.

"Uncle Jack?"

I smiled. "Yes. He knows everything."

"Your uncle is epic." Christy bit her nail. "I wish I had an uncle like that, but my uncle is in prison."

"Well, that's quite special too," I said. "I'm sure not many children have an uncle who's in prison."

I was actually desperate to ask what her uncle had done (a burglary or murder or maybe a bank robbery), but I wasn't sure if it was the polite thing to do.

"If we were going out together," Christy continued, "Uncle Jack would sort of be my uncle too, wouldn't he?"

I was sure she was joking so I began to laugh hysterically. But then she ran off and started talking to Anna and Florence, and I saw Anna and Florence looking at me angrily.

What had I done now? Perhaps I should email Uncle Jack.

From: Sam Billington
To: Uncle Jack
Subject: Dinos

Hi Uncle Jack,

We've just watched a film with our class about dinosaurs that come back to life. (There was a bit of dinosaur blood in a rock.)

Could that really happen?
Could someone breed a new dinosaur from dinosaur blood?

A girl from my class asked. (Christy)

From: Professor Jack Scott McNeil
To: Sam Billington
Subject: Re: Dinos

Great question! I take it you watched *Jurassic Park* – by the way, that's far too scary, even though it is rated PG :-)

But in order to answer your question: no, that's probably not possible. It's over 65 million years ago that the dinosaurs were around. That's too long for DNA to survive. We've only been finding dinosaur skeletons (not blood). And even if you did find a bit of blood with DNA in, it would be so damaged that you'd never be able to decipher it and use it.

Also: we don't have any dinosaur eggs that we could use for breeding dinosaurs. You could of course use an ostrich egg, but I'm not sure that this would be successful.

I do think it might be possible to bring back to life animals that became extinct a lot more recently. Dodos, for instance. You know, those stocky birds that used to live on the island of Mauritius. They became extinct 300 years ago because Dutch sailors ate them all.

Or perhaps mammoths. Woolly mammoths only died out 4,000 years ago. But I don't think we'll ever be able to see living dinosaurs (except in movies). So you can reassure your girlfriend.

Best wishes,
Uncle Jack

From: Sam Billington
To: Uncle Jack
Subject: Re: Dinos

Thanks.

PS: Christy isn't my girlfriend.

WEDNESDAY

"If you pick the flatworm," said Archie, "I'll go for the chimpanzee."

"The flatworm?" I said. "Why don't YOU do the flatworm! You're the one who likes snakes."

"Yes, I do like snakes, but not flatworms. Flatworms are stupid."

Archie picked up the iPad and started Googling. "Hey, look at this! Flatworms eat with their bottoms."

"Or they poo with their mouths," I said. "Depending on how you put it."

"Sir!" Florence was waving her arms. "Archie and Sam are being disgusting!"

Mr Nolan came over and bent forwards. "Archie and Sam. Can you get to work, please?"

"We ARE working!" I protested.

"Not true, Sir!" cried Florence. "They're looking up pictures of totally gross worms! Who eat with their bottoms."

"Yes. Because we have to RESEARCH them!"

It was morning and we were all working at the picnic tables next to our tent. Mr Nolan had given us all small, blue notebooks. He called them passports. In each passport he had stuck two animals; we were the research scientists and had to find out our animals' characteristics.

Archie and I had been given chimpanzee and flatworm. I think flatworms are the most stupid animals you could ever come up with – they don't even have legs! They don't have brains, either! If you had brains you wouldn't eat with your bottom. I'd much rather do a platypus or an acanthodes (a really cool spiny shark, sadly extinct now) but we weren't allowed to swap animals and Archie had already started on his chimpanzee, so I had no choice but to look into the flatworm and its characteristics: a head and a mouth and kidneys and DNA and an intestinal tube.

Those are all things chimpanzees have, too. But chimpanzees

also have a skull and teeth and a jaw and lungs. And a brain. And fingers and toes. And a thumb which can move in any direction. Only monkeys and people have that.

"When you're ready, add your findings to the big poster," Mr Nolan said.

"Hey, look!" said Archie.

"That's weird!" said Christy.

The rest of the class were playing football, but Archie, Christy, Anna, and I were looking at the poster Mr Nolan had stuck onto the tent.

We had researched a lot of different animals. Bacteria. Flatworms. Lancet fish. Sharks. Reptiles. Platypuses. Apes. Humans. There were many similarities between them. It looked like they were all related, somehow. Only, there was a scale of complexity and lots of variety.

Bacteria.

Bacteria with tails.

A flatworm.

Fish with gills.

Fish with lungs, which could also survive out of the water.

Fish with fins that were also used as legs.

Animals that were able to live in the water and on land.

Reptiles.

Mammals.

"It looks as if they are all connected, as if they have a common ancestor," I said.

Anna clicked her tongue, just like Mum does when I drop a jam jar onto the floor. "That may SEEM so," she said. "But it isn't. It wouldn't be possible for a monkey to emerge from a fish. If I lock up my hamster long enough it won't turn into a human being."

No. She was right.

"The theory of evolution hasn't even been proven. It's just a theory," she concluded.

"Come on," Archie said. "Let's go and play some football, Sam. I'll teach you all about defending."

"I'll come in a minute," I said. "I just want to send one more email."

From: Sam Billington
To: Uncle Jack
Subject: Not proven

Hi Uncle,

Is it true that the theory of evolution hasn't been proven?? Because it's just a theory? That's what Anna says.

From: Professor Jack Scott McNeil
To: Sam Billington
Subject: Re: Not proven

No, that's not true.

It has been proven that animal and plant species were formed through a long process of evolution. In the first three billion years there were only teeny-weeny living beings: single-cell organisms.

And in the past half a billion years all bigger species of animals and plants have evolved. There is no doubt anymore that this happened, really. There are countless indications of this from different fields of science. You can see it in fossils. You can see it in DNA. Time and time again it is confirmed: the theory of evolution is sound. Rock solid.

And so "theory" doesn't mean it's just a nice idea!

Have a look at this video called "A history of the Earth": www.faradayschools.com/primary/charles-darwin-spotting-science-in-nature/

Cheers,
Uncle Jack

From: Sam Billington
To: Uncle Jack
Subject: Re: Not proven

But if you lock an animal away for a very long time, let's say an elephant – could it change into a different species? Can we test if the evolution theory works?

From: Professor Jack Scott McNeil
To: Sam Billington
Subject: Re: Not proven

Yes, that's possible. You can lock up a family of elephants and wait until they've changed into a different species. But you'd need to be extremely patient. And wait for about a hundred million years...

It takes a while before an elephant can have a baby: twelve years! And the baby will look quite like its mum and dad. Evolution works in very small steps.

If you wanted to watch evolution at work, you'd be better off using bacteria. A bacterium can split into two daughters after no less than twenty minutes. After forty minutes a bacterium already has four granddaughters. And after one hour she's a great-granny of eight little ones! After twelve hours there'll be over 68 billion great-great-great-great-great grandchildren. And those are likely to be a bit different from their great-great-great-great-great granny, as bacteria evolve.

Do you remember that Auntie Janet was really ill last winter? (Probably not.) She was suffering from a throat infection, and the GP gave her a medicine that would kill the bacteria in her throat: antibiotics.

But it didn't do anything. Auntie Janet kept having a sore throat.

Antibiotics kill most bacteria. But sometimes there's one bacterium that changes a tiny little bit, and it won't be affected. This bacterium just carries on splitting, despite the antibiotics. So your throat infection doesn't go away!

These changing bacteria pose a real problem for doctors!

From: Sam Billington
To: Uncle Jack
Subject: Re: Not proven

So Auntie Janet is living proof of how sound the theory of evolution
is ☺

From: Professor Jack Scott McNeil
To: Sam Billington
Subject: Re: Not proven

Exactly!

WEDNESDAY AFTERNOON

This afternoon we went to Newcastle, to a large, round cinema in the Life Science Centre. It has the biggest planetarium in the north of England. We were the ONLY people there, and we were all given 3D-glasses, and we could lie back on massive armchairs in a dome. It felt like being inside a giant half-football. It was super chilled.

The inside of the football was all screen. It felt as if we were outside, on the moors, gazing at the sky. The light around us gradually faded. The sun went down and it got darker and darker until all we could see was stars. They moved from left to right across the sky, as if time was ticking ten times faster than usual. And there was a man in a spacesuit who told us that we were all going to the moon, and we had to count down from ten to one, and then he started the engine, and we lifted off in the rocket, super fast, and the Earth became smaller and smaller, and the moon got closer and closer, so close that I stretched out my arm because I thought I would be able to grab it, but I couldn't. We carried on flying, to Mars and Saturn, and even further, all the way past the Milky Way, and the stars were zooming past like embers escaping from a fire.

"Sir," Florence groaned. "I'm feeling a bit sick."

"OK. Take your glasses off and shut your eyes for a few minutes," Mr Nolan said.

"That doesn't help!"

"Does anyone have a plastic bag for Florence?" Mr Nolan asked.

And we flew back, from the Milky Way to Saturn, on to Mars and back to Earth again. When we'd finally landed on Earth, I felt quite relieved.

The universe is really quite big.

"Now then," Mr Nolan said when we'd finished doing the dishes – Mr Nolan, Mehmet and Rachid had made pasta bolognaise and this time there were no kitchen disasters. I ate three platefuls! – "Tonight we're going to do something really fun."

"Musical chairs!" shouted Florence. "And the boys are the chairs!"

Archie and I looked at each other. Live musical chairs. That was a terrible idea. Thankfully the other boys thought the same.

"Why don't we play Tinker Tailor or the camouflage game?" said Matteo.

"Yes, or football," Tom said.

Mr Nolan waved a stack of paper in the air. "We're going to do a treasure hunt. In the woods."

"Oh no, Sir. No, please."

"Can we choose to not play, Sir?"

"No, we're all going to take part," said Mr Nolan. "And you'll hand in your mobile phones first."

Florence shook her head. "I am not handing you my phone, Sir."

"My mum said I always have to keep my mobile on me," Esther said.

"What are you going to do with them, Sir?" Matteo asked. "With our phones? You aren't going to call Monica, are you?" Monica is Mr Nolan's girlfriend, who's moved to the States for a few months. Mr Nolan is madly in love with her and they're getting married next year.

Mr Nolan laughed. "No, of course I won't use your phones. I promise. I'll give them to Tony, and he'll look after them. But we'll be doing the treasure hunt in a very special area: the International Dark Sky Park.[9] There's an open-air gallery with large telescopes which receive radio waves from space. If you were walking around with your mobile phones..."

---

9 For a cool video about the International Dark Sky Park in Northumberland, and the Kielder Observatory, visit: www. visitnorthumberland.com/darkskies

"... they might think they'd found aliens!" said Matteo.

"Yes, and when they went out to explore they'd find YOU," Archie said.

"And we wouldn't want that," Mr Nolan said. "Just in case they send you off to Mars, Matteo."

Matteo punched his fist in the air. "Yeeeah!"

"And then what would I say to your mum?" Mr Nolan went around with a washing-up bowl. "All phones in here, please."

"But Sir!" Anna crossed her arms. "What if something happened..."

"Nothing will happen. The area is totally safe."

"What about wolves? The wolves that roam the area?"

Mr Nolan chuckled. "They're more afraid of you than you are of them. They would never go anywhere near a noisy bunch like you. And anyway, how could your phone help you if you bumped into a wolf?"

"You could throw your phone at it!" said Matteo. He pretended to throw his mobile at a wolf and accidentally flung it against a tree trunk. "Whoops! Oh, it's fine. It's still working."

"We'll be going in small groups," Mr Nolan said. "And if you feel scared, you can come with me. I've got a brown belt in judo. I once broke someone's collarbone."

Florence tutted. "Sir. You shouldn't be proud of that!"

"I'm not proud of it. It was an accident. I was just telling you so you know I'm very strong. OK. Groups of four, please."

"Sam, let's go together!" Archie said.

"I'll go with you," Matteo said. "Come on, Christy. We'll go with Sam and Archie."

We were the last group to leave.

I don't like walking. But the dark sky reserve was amazing. Especially the outdoor planet trail they'd set out for the summer. We were supposed to walk the trail and end up at the Sky Space, and then carry on to the observatory before we headed back to the campsite. The trail was like a walk through space. With every step we took, we covered 2.5 million kilometres! And there are planets everywhere, even if they're quite far apart.

We started with Pluto. Pluto didn't really belong to the planet trail, as technically it's not a planet anymore. It's a bit sad to leave Pluto out though, because it used to be part of the planets. On the trail, Pluto was a bit like a beetle pinned up behind a glass frame. It was a really teeny-weeny-weeny planet, and we then had to walk a really long way to get to Neptune, the next planet, which was only the size of a marble.

And then there was nothing for a long time.

"I bet this is Luke and Tom's doing," Christy moaned. "They probably nicked the planets for fun. It can't be this far to the next planet."

"It's sooo boring in space," Archie complained. "The planets are really too far apart. If you had to go there for real, you'd be dead by the time you got there."

"Oh look!" shouted Matteo. "A climbing tree!" He sprinted into the woods and climbed the tree.

"Can you see another planet?" I asked. "Can you see Uranus?"

Matteo shook his head. "I can't see a thing. Just trees." He climbed a bit higher. "No, wait. There! There's something!"

He quickly came down from the tree and ran ahead of us. It

looked like he was going a billion miles an hour. Between the trees, something was glistening in the last light of day.

A planet?

No, it was a small bridge. A bridge with a weight on. You could lift it to find out what ten litres of water feels like on Earth. And a bit further down there was another bridge, where you could lift a weight to find out what ten litres of water would feel like on the moon.

It was as light as a feather. On the moon I'd be as strong as a horse. Archie was standing next to the Jupiter bridge and tried to pull the weight. "This is impossible to lift. Way too heavy!" he panted. "I'm glad we don't live on Jupiter."

"Come on," Christy said. She glanced at the sky and looked a bit worried. The sun had gone down, and its light was fading. "We've got to carry on. Otherwise we won't be back before it gets dark."

"Let's run!" Matteo shot off like an arrow. We found him a few billion miles further down the path, next to a type of satellite dish. If you whispered into the dish, you could be heard 50 metres away, on the other side of a pond, where there was another dish. I went over to the other dish, and suddenly I heard Matteo's voice. It felt as if he was whispering in my ear.

"Hey Sam! There's a wolf behind you."

Of course I knew it wasn't true, but I accidentally turned around anyway. Matteo started laughing hysterically right into the dish, and into my ear. "Hahaha!"

"DON'T BE SO STUPID," I shouted into the dish.

"Ouch!" Matteo grabbed his ears and jumped up and down. "My eardrum! You burst my eardrum!"

"IT'S YOUR OWN FAULT!"

"What? WHAT DID YOU SAY? I can't hear you! My ears have stopped working."

"Come on guys, are you coming or not?" Christy called. "We have to hurry. What does it say on the sheet? I can't read it anymore!"

I ran down the hill. It was pretty dark by now. Especially in the woods. The evening bird calls were getting louder and louder and the tops of the pine trees were swishing noisily to and fro in the wind, just like waves crashing onto the beach. Matteo kept running ahead and then returning.

"Jupiter! I've found Jupiter! Come quickly!"

"Mars! There's Mars! Come on, guys. We're nearly there!"

"Hey Sam, you won't believe this! The Earth turns as fast as 300 metres per second! So if you stand still, you're actually still running! Wait. Posts. Hey. Where do these posts lead to? I'll have a look."

No, please don't, I wanted to say. But he'd already gone.

Into the woods.

We carried on, towards the sun.

"I wonder where Matteo is," said Christy, when we reached Earth.

"He's been away for quite a long time now," Archie said.

We called his name. "Matteo!"

"Where are you?"

"Hey, Matteo, this isn't funny anymore!"

"Come on!"

But Matteo didn't come. I got a tight feeling in my tummy.

"Come on," said Christy. "Let's go and find him."

"OK," said Archie. "And when we've found him, we'll beat him up."

"He went into the woods somewhere over there," I said. "Near Mars. MATTEO!"

"Where the white posts are," said Christy. "But where are the white posts? I can't see anything anymore."

"Here!" said Archie. "I found one. Come on. MATTEO!"

The white posts didn't form a path. They'd just been put randomly in between the bushes. We had to squeeze through, branches slapping me in the face, and I felt horrid sticky twigs pushing me back.

It was really dark now. The birds had stopped singing. All you could hear was the rustling of the pine trees.

"Matteo!"

No answer. "I can't see any more posts," Christy said. We were now in the middle of the wood. It was pitch black.

Archie cupped his hands around his mouth. "Hey. Matteo! Game over. Come back!"

We stopped. We listened. And then we heard it.

Growling.

My heart skipped a beat. I thought of the wolves. The wolves roaming the area. The wolves that wouldn't hurt a fly. At least, as long as they weren't hungry...

"I'm a bit scared," whispered Christy. She clasped her hand in mine.

"I'm not," I said. I tried to swallow but my throat felt dry. "I'm not scared at all. Don't worry, these woods are very safe."

Rustling in the bushes. Snapping branches. Growling. Panting.

Christy squeezed my fingers. I stepped backwards.

And then, all of a sudden, something black jumped out of the bushes. I was so startled by it that I fell over backwards. Something jumped out on top of me. Something really heavy.

Then I heard Matteo's voice whisper in my ear: "Haha! I tricked you! You all thought I was a wolf!"

I pushed him away. "I didn't think that. Get off me!"

"Matteo!" Christy's voice sounded very angry. "That wasn't funny!"

"Hahaha! I think it's very funny!" laughed Matteo. "I'll never get over how funny it was!"

"It's extremely late!" Archie said. "And it's all because of you."

I got onto my feet. "Yes. And now we've missed the observatory."

"Who cares? This was so much better! Why would you want to visit a bunch of boring telescopes!"

"Well, I'd have loved to see some black holes!" I said.

BLACK HOLES

Imagine a monster vacuum cleaner which is SO powerful that it sucks you up. Whatever you do, whatever you try to hold on to, you can't escape. You are sucked into the tube! And you can never get back out!

SPAGHETTI

A black hole is a bit like a monster vacuum cleaner. It attracts everything within its reach, sucks it up, and never lets it go again. If you were floating in space with your spacesuit on and accidentally got near a black hole, you'd go right in, and you'd be stretched out into a long strand of spaghetti. Once you were sucked up, you could never escape. Nothing can escape from a black hole. Not even light. That's because of its extremely strong gravitational force.

ORIGIN

How does a black hole come into being?

When a star becomes old, it runs out of fuel. It collapses. Then the outside of the star is blown apart by the force of the explosion, and the inside becomes a black hole.

A black hole is absolutely teeny-weeny, but it is VERY powerful and VERY heavy. Make sure you don't get anywhere near it!

"Which way do we go now?" asked Christy.

It was silent for a moment. I had no idea which direction we had to go in. We had strayed off the path, and the white posts were nowhere to be seen.

"I think we came that way," said Archie.

"No. It was definitely that way," said Matteo. "I'm sure it was. Come on."

I sighed. Christy and I trailed behind Archie and Matteo.

I peered ahead of me. Somewhere in this wood was the planet trail. And if we found that, we'd know which way to go. But there wasn't a path. There were just trees. And bushes. And a ditch we couldn't cross. We had to go back again.

The pine trees were swaying so wildly in the wind that we could hardly hear each other's voices, and it was cold. Only my left hand wasn't cold, because Christy was holding it firmly.

"I wish I had my phone," said Christy. "I could have used it as a torch."

"I wish I had my phone," shouted Archie, trying to be heard above the noise of the wind. "So I could switch on Google Maps and find out where we are."

"AND I WOULD JUST CALL MR NOLAN," shouted Matteo. "TO TELL HIM TO COME AND GET US."

The ground turned soft again. The trees disappeared. We were walking across a sandy area, just like a very cold desert.

"I've got sand in my shoes," Matteo said. He stood still and looked around. "Does anyone know where we are?"

"No idea," Archie said. "Perhaps we'll need to stay here all night."

"No!" shouted Christy. "I don't want to stay here all night!"

"Maybe we should build a shelter," said Matteo. "That's what Bear Grylls does all the time. In the wild."

"Shut up," said Archie.

"I'll make a fire," he went on. "I know how to do that. You just need a stick and you've got to twist it very fast, until it's warm and then—"

"No way," Christy said. "I'm not going to sleep here, Matteo!"

I looked up at the sky. The clouds were moving along very fast, concealing the moon on and off.

"And we'll build a trap," Matteo continued. "Maybe we can shoot a rabbit first."

The gap in the clouds was getting bigger. I gazed at the stars. And suddenly I saw it. The "saucepan". The Great Bear.

Hang on. If I knew where the Great Bear was, I would also know where the North Star was, also called Polaris.

"Look!" I shouted. I pointed at the sky. "There! North is that way. Come on, guys. We have to go this way."

"What?" said Archie.

"Do you know where we are?" Matteo pushed me so hard that I nearly fell over.

"Well, hmm," I said. "At least I know which way to go."

Christy threw her arms around me and hugged me so tightly that I could barely breathe. "Woohoo!"

"Uhmm…" I said, taking a step back. "It's actually really simple. All you need to do is find Polaris, and then you know."

Christy shook her head and sighed. "Wow. That's so cool."

Archie patted me on the shoulder. "Sam, you're SUCH an epic science geek."

We crossed the sandy area and arrived back at the woods. It was a very long walk and we had to keep stopping because Christy had a stone in her shoe, and Matteo had a blister and I wanted to look at the stars through the treetops, to make sure we were still heading in the right direction.

"Are you sure we're going the right way?" asked Christy.

"I could climb a tree," said Matteo. "Maybe I can see the road."

"That won't be necessary," I said, because I saw the flickering of car headlights in the distance.

"There's the road." At last. There was the car park. In the distance I saw the lights of the farm.

When we were nearly at the campsite we all started running. Mr Nolan and Tony were standing in front of the farmhouse. They were holding big torches. They were just about to come and find us.

"Sir!" Matteo panted. "We're back!"

"Guys!" Mr Nolan called out. "Where on earth have you been?!"

I cleared my throat. We weren't going to tell him it was all Matteo's fault.

"Uhmm... We lost our way."

"But Sam saved us!" said Christy. She squeezed my hand. "He just looked at the stars. And then he knew which way to go."

"So, does that mean you're finally going out?" enquired Florence.

I shook my head. "No."

"Yes," said Christy.

"Well, okay then," I said.

THURSDAY

"Ladies and gentlemen, this is your tour leader speaking," Mr Nolan announced into the microphone. "I hope you are enjoying your comfy seats and the wonderful views. We are nearly in Newcastle now and…"

Matteo, who was facing away from us in order to wave at the cars behind us, turned around, threw his arms in the air and sang, "Are we nearly there yet? Hey, are we nearly there yet?"

"There's something I'd briefly like to discuss with you."

"Are we nearly there yet? Gotta keep busy… rock, paper, scissors… are we there yet?"

Mr Nolan raised his hand. "Nice song, Matteo, but just hold on a minute. I want to talk us through our plan for the day."

Plan for the day?

"So today we're going to the Hancock Museum of Natural History and we'll be finding out as much as possible about how life on Earth began."

Anna sniffed. "According to people who don't believe in God."

"According to science," I said.

"Stupid geek," Tom murmured, so quietly that nobody but me heard.

"Who knows what it means not to be prejudiced?" asked Mr Nolan.

"That you don't have any favourites!" Florence called out.

"It means," Mr Nolan said, "that you wait to make up your mind until you have sufficient knowledge. So you don't immediately shout 'This is wrong!' Or 'It's against the Bible!' It means that first of all you gather information and try to learn and understand as much as possible. Only then do you start to reflect: What do I think about this? Is it true? Do I agree? First we'll have a guided tour. But then you're allowed to complete your own tasks. I want you to act like detectives. Go around the museum and investigate any clues you can find. We're going to try to find out if the theory of evolution makes sense. You're going to go around in groups of four. Each group will have an important research task. In a minute I will give you each an envelope with a secret mission."

"I'm going with Tom!" Luke said quickly. "Rachid and Mehmet, you'll join us, won't you?" The four of them bumped fists. "We'll find clues that it's all nonsense. Evolution."

Matteo put his arms around me and nearly squeezed me to death. "We're going together. Archie, you're in too."

Christy turned around. "Sam! I'm going with you!"

"Here are your secret missions," Mr Nolan said. I tore open our envelope.

Try to find out as much as possible about Charles Darwin.

"What have we got?" said Matteo. "Let's see. What's our secret mission? Try to find out as much as possible about..."

I quickly put my hand over his mouth. "Ssshhh. Don't say a thing."

"Why not! Why can't I say it? Charles Dar—"

"Because it's a secret mission."

"Oh. Hey, Christy! We have to find out who Charles Darwin is!"

Sigh.

We finally arrived at the Hancock Museum of Natural History in Newcastle. The sun was shining, and it was quite a walk from the coach park to the museum entrance, which wouldn't have been too bad if it weren't for the cool box with dead animals in, which Matteo and I were hauling along. It felt heavier every step we took.

"Keep up the pace, boys!" Mr Nolan called out. He clapped his hands together. "Come on, Sam. Come on, Matteo! Speed up!"

"Sir!" I panted. "Do you have any idea how heavy this thing is?"

"It'll make your muscles stronger. Chop chop!"

A lady in a light blue shirt was waiting for us on the grand steps in front of the museum. "Trinity School?" she asked.

"Yes," Mr Nolan said. "This way, guys!"

By the time Matteo and I had staggered up the steep steps, we'd run out of steam completely. We let go of the cool box. My hands were burning.

"Ah, you've brought your own food and drink," said the lady in the light blue shirt. "Very organized."

Matteo shook his head. "No. This isn't food. This is uhmm... for you." He unclipped the lid of the cool box and opened it up.

The lady glanced inside. The colour drained from her face and she sprang back in horror. "What is THAT?! It's disgusting!"

"These are our dead animals," Archie explained.

I rubbed my hands together. "We collected them," I said.

"As payment for our entrance fees." Archie looked into the entrance hall. "Is Steve Backshall here?"

The lady shook her head. "Please remove this cool box at once!"

"Where shall we take it?" I asked. I looked around to see if there was a desk for handing in dead animals.

"No idea," the lady said, shortly. "I don't mind where you take it. As long as you get it away from me."

"Maybe she's new here," Rachid said to me. "Excuse me, Miss. These animals are for you. So you can stuff them and display them in the museum. We'd like to exchange them for entrance tickets."

An older gentleman with glasses and a light blue museum shirt came out towards us. "You may now go into the hall, through the glass doors into the cloakroom. You can leave your coats and backpacks and then I'd like you to—"

169

"Excuse me, John?" said the lady. "This group has brought a cool box with dead rats in."

"Moles," I said. "And a few mice."

"And three baby rabbits," Archie added. "But it wasn't me who killed them – they were already dead."

Rachid raised his hand. "And a budgie. A really awesome one. Would you like to see him?"

John lifted the lid off the cool box. He slowly shook his head.

"This is very kind of you, but I'm afraid these are of no use to us here."

Mr Nolan took a step forwards. "I do apologize. It was our understanding that we would receive a free entrance ticket for an educational visit. In exchange for a dead animal."

John shook his head. "No, I'm sorry. That must have been a misunderstanding."

"What?" shouted Rachid. "But Matteo told us!"

Everyone looked at Matteo.

Matteo stared at the floor. He scratched a scab on his arm. "I thought we could..." he said softly.

"You said it was written on a sign!" said Anna.

"Yes," said Matteo. His shoulders drooped.

For a moment, it was quiet.

"Smart move," Luke said. "So we collected all those dead animals for nothing. Cheers, Matteo."

I can get quite fed up with Matteo, too. Last night for example, when he'd hidden in the woods, I was really grumpy. But not now. I only felt cross with Luke. I could feel the anger rising up inside me like a hot flash of lightning. "You didn't even collect anything!" I said. "So you can stop moaning. OK?"

"WHAT did you say?" Luke said in a menacing voice.

"That you can stop moaning. Right now!"

Luke moved towards me. I moved towards him. I looked at Luke, my eyes half shut. Luke took a step back. He tripped over a stone and nearly fell off the steps. Mr Nolan just managed to grab him.

"Calm down, boys, please," he said. "We're going to sort this out right now. So if I understand it correctly, we can't uhmm… get rid of these animals here?'

John shook his head. "No, I'm sorry. I am terribly sorry."

"Then we have a bit of a problem."

A new school group was coming up the steps. They didn't have a cool box and were allowed to walk straight through the door.

Matteo tugged gently at Mr Nolan's sleeve. He was blinking. "Sir. I have some money. Here." He pressed a ten-pound note into his hand.

I quickly rummaged in my bag. I had brought some money, too. My mum had given me ten pounds spending money, and twenty pounds in case of emergency. And this was very clearly an emergency.

"I've got fifteen pounds," Archie said.

"And here's twenty quid," Christy said.

Mr Nolan shook his head. "Thank you, children, but there is no need. I have the money. That's not the issue. Put the ten pounds back in your wallet, please, Matteo. And you too, Christy. It's not needed. No, my problem now is where to leave the dead animals. Is there anywhere here we can get rid of them?"

"Bury them," Anna said, indignant. "We can't throw them away. We have to give them a proper burial!"

"You can't get rid of the animals here," said John. "And you can't bury them, either. We're in the middle of a student campus in the city."

"All right," Mr Nolan said. "We'll just have to take them back to our campsite. That's our only option, I think."

Luke nudged Tom. "Great. We'll have a BBQ tonight."

Mr Nolan scowled. "We'll take them back and organize a proper funeral. Please could we leave our cool box here for a few hours? I promise we'll take it back with us."

"That's fine with me," said John. And then I overheard him whispering to Mr Nolan. "You know what? We usually charge school groups. But I'm happy to let you all go in for free today, as you've gone to a lot of trouble with your dead rats."

"Really?" Mr Nolan's face lit up. "That's fantastic!"

"Just keep it to yourself."

"I will," Mr Nolan said. "Come on, everyone!"

At last we were allowed in.

"Steve!" shouted Archie. "Sam, look! Steve Backshall!"

It was true. There was Steve Backshall in his T-shirt and shorts, standing on top of a large cabinet in the hall. This was our lucky day! At least, that's what we thought. Then we realized he was made of cardboard.

We followed John through the hall and into the gallery, where we saw lots of stuffed animals, including a polar bear called Eric, and lots of cardboard Steve Backshalls, too. It was a large area full of epic creatures. I knew at once that this was the most awesome museum in the WORLD. It felt a bit like Charlie's amazing chocolate factory, except there were no chocolate rivers or Oompa Loompas, but dinosaur fossils and skeletons – some extremely tall, like the T-Rex – and there was a mammoth with tusks that looked like the forks of a fork-lift truck. But there were also jellyfish and octopuses in large glass jars, beetles and butterflies pinned up on the walls, and a monster crab called a Giant Japanese Spider Crab, which had made even the Queen gasp when she visited the museum.

"That's not a real crab," said Luke.

"It IS a real crab," said Archie.

"Carry on walking!" John called out, and he took us to the archives, a room with lots of drawers and cabinets full of animals, all dead and stuffed or pinned up. We were allowed to have a quick peek.

"Please can we have a proper look inside?" Archie asked.

Sadly we weren't allowed. Only scientists were allowed in. So we carried on to the next room, with even more stuffed animals. We met Sparkie the Budgie, a stuffed budgerigar-turned-television star that had won a speaking bird contest in 1958.

Rachid gulped. Sparkie reminded him of his own dead budgie.

We went on to the fossils in the Fossil Stories room. There we saw trilobites which looked like woodlice but had actually been around before the dinosaurs. There were amphibians and fish fossils and a model of a pterodactyl. And there were fish with lungs so they could breathe when the river had dried out, and fish with legs, so they could crawl onto dry land when a predator fish was trying to eat them.

John explained that all the fossils were a bit like different shots from a single film. You could see how different species had come into being. From very simple animals to very complex ones.[10]

RACEHORSE

If you visit tinyurl.com/firstfilmever or scan the code, you can watch a video of a galloping horse. It's actually a rather dull video: it only takes a few seconds, it's black and white and there's no

 sound whatsoever. And yet it's very special. This video was made in 1878, and it's the first video that was ever filmed. If you look carefully, you can see some numbers in the bottom left corner, ranging from 1 to 16.

The film is actually made of sixteen photos which were taken in very quick succession. If you show the photographs very quickly one after the other, it looks just as if the horse is really galloping. For a longer film you'd need tens of thousands of images, of course.

Also watch: tinyurl.com/earlyfilmmaking and learn more about early film-making.

The evolution theory is a bit like an old black and white film. But one with lots of missing images. A hundred years ago we'd only found a few shots from the film. But the longer we kept on searching, the more images we found. And what's really special is that all these separate images belong to the same film. You can just insert them in the right place.

Many of the images are still missing. But from the shots we already have, we get an idea of what the overall film is like. This is how life has evolved.

JIGSAW

Imagine that right in front of you is a 1,000-piece jigsaw puzzle. You're excited about making it, but before you even get started, your little brother gets his hands on it. He scatters the pieces around the room. You get cross at your annoying little brother and *try to sort out the pieces. But before you know it, the dog eats some of them. And then your dad vacuums some more. And your little brother sneakily slips some in the bin.*

Infuriating! Your jigsaw can no longer be completed. But most of the pieces are still there and they fit together perfectly. Despite the missing bits you can still make out what the picture looks like.

The theory of evolution is a bit like a jigsaw with missing pieces. It's too bad you haven't got all the pieces. But the pieces you do have only fit together in one particular way. And they fit so perfectly that you can be sure that it has to be right. It would have been impossible to put the jigsaw together in any other way.

The best thing was that we all got our own fossil. We were allowed to chisel it out of a stone, and then we could clean off the dust with a brush. And then we had to weigh it. In my stone was a shell which used to be home to a little squid. We were allowed to take our fossil home.

This was the BEST DAY EVER!!

And then, at last, we were free to explore by ourselves. We had to find the secret clues. Our mission was to find out as much as possible about Charles Darwin. We had no idea where to go, so we went back to the gallery. There were massive tree trunks, lots of stuffed animals and even some live ones, including a wolf fish and some lizards and pythons. Just when we were about to carry on, I heard a voice behind us. "Charles Darwin was allowed to sail on a ship," the voice said.

I turned round. There was a man teaching a group of older children. About Charles Darwin.

That was lucky! All we had to do was eavesdrop!

Charles Darwin

SCREAMING PATIENTS

Darwin was a bit of a difficult child. He was very clever, no problem there. But he wouldn't make any effort at school. So Darwin's dad took necessary measures.

"With this letter I am informing you that I am taking my child out of school. He is a poor and miserable student.
He only cares about dogs, shooting, and rat catching. He is a disgrace to our family!"

What do you do with a child who gets very low marks, doesn't pay attention during lessons, and is terribly lazy? Just send him to medical school, of course! It's a no-brainer.

But there was a problem. Darwin didn't like blood. And he lived in a time before painkillers, so patients were fully conscious during surgery, which meant that they screamed hysterically during operations. Charles Darwin's time at university was a disaster.

But his dad was not deterred. Charles would have to become a vicar. Vicars don't have to operate, and there are no screaming patients to put them off.

But oh dear. Charles wasn't interested in becoming a vicar. He preferred collecting beetles with his cousin. Nature. That's what Charles Darwin was interested in.

Would you like to join me on a trip around the world?

When he was 22 years old, Darwin received a very special invitation. "Would you like to join me on a trip around the world?" asked captain Robert Fitzroy. "I have to make maps and think I'll

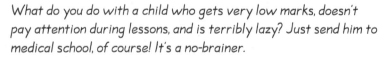

be away for quite some time. If you come with me, at least I'll have someone to talk to."

The trip took five years. Poor Charles. He couldn't stand sailing. The poor man was constantly seasick. Except when they went ashore. Charles Darwin had the time of his life when they went on land. He could study nature, and he saw some incredible things. Giant turtles, swimming lizards, and strange birds.

BIZARRE BIRDS

Charles Darwin discovered something he'd read about before: that the Earth is very old. And that life had changed over time. How did he work this out? On different islands Darwin came across birds, first mockingbirds and then later finches, that looked somewhat similar but still different. They had very different bills, different colours, and they ate different food.

Were they related? Or were they completely different species?

ADAPTATION OR EXTINCTION

On each island Darwin collected a few finches, which he took back to the boat. Dead finches. Later on someone told him that all these finches were related. But then why did they have such different bills? The islands he visited were quite different from one another. On one island there were trees with hard seeds, whereas another island had more trees with soft seeds. The finches on the hard-seed island had large, strong beaks: just thick enough to crack open the hard seeds. And on the soft-seed island the finches had smaller beaks. And yet another group of finches had handy pointed, beetle-finding beaks.

Of course a bird can't just put on a different beak when it wants to. But birds do have babies. Children look like their parents but there are differences, too. You don't look exactly like your mum or dad. Maybe you have a different nose, or maybe you'll grow taller. It's the same for birds. Perhaps in one nest of finches there's one baby with a different beak. A beak that's a bit more thin and pointy. That beak is just slightly better for finding insects. On an island where the main food source is insects, that bird will be better adapted to life than the other finches. The finches with the less useful, thick beaks can't find food as easily. They die out. The finches with the thin, pointy beaks are able to get more insects. Thanks to decent, filling meals, they'll have enough energy to build a nest. They'll then have babies with the same pointy beaks. And the baby bird with the most pointy beak will have the most chance to outwit his siblings when looking for food. This bird will have babies, too.

And after fifty or a hundred years you'll find only pointy-beak finches on the beetle island.

KICKBOXING FROGS

Have you ever watched two frogs fighting?

Probably not. Frogs don't hit and kick or bite each other. And yet they do fight.

A female frog may lay 2,500 eggs at a time. Imagine that all those eggs hatched and turned into frogs! And that the following year, all female frogs became mothers again of 2,500 frogs each. Within a few years you'd have a terrible plague of frogs. Frogs in your bedroom, frogs in your bed, frogs in the toilet. Frogs would rule the world.

But most tadpoles don't make it into frogs. Either they're eaten up or they can't find enough food to survive. Only the strongest frogs survive. The frogs that are best at finding food. The fastest, smartest, strongest frogs win the fight for survival. And only those frogs will have babies.

Charles Darwin discovered that animal species can gradually change over time.

Hey, he thought, but if that's the case, they could also change into other species. That's how animal species must have come into being. From very simple cells, into aquatic animals, into fish, into amphibians, into mammals...

BANG!

Charles Darwin didn't find it easy to tell people in England about his ideas. He felt it was as challenging as it would be to confess a murder. He thought people would be really angry with him. Because that's not what the Bible says, surely?

And he was right: some people were upset about his ideas. And some people laughed at him. But there were also people who thought: interesting, this could be true!

PROOF

The thing scientists enjoy most is shooting down each other's theories. To see if they can disprove them. To see if they can stand the test, or if they collapse under the weight of further investigation. Of course that's exactly what happened to Charles Darwin's ideas! Darwin could come up with anything, really... But was it true?

After 150 years of further investigation it has become clear that Charles was right. This can be demonstrated in several different ways.

Fossils are remains or imprints preserved in rock of animals, plants, and other organisms that lived a long time ago. Some very special fossils have been discovered. For example:
- The Tiktaalik: a fish with small arms that could crawl onto land

- *The Archaeopteryx: a real dino – but with feathers and wings. One of the first birds! Fossils like these show that some fish have changed into land animals. And some dinosaurs evolved into birds.*

Every cell has a computer programme: DNA. When Charles was alive, he'd never heard of DNA, but nowadays we are able to decode it. And what have we discovered? That all living things are related. Plants. Grass. Animals. Humans. You can create a whole family tree. A family tree which shows that this is how some species have evolved from other species.

There are still finches on the islands once visited by Darwin. Biologists have been keeping a close eye on these finches for years now. And they've found that the birds are still adapting! If there isn't much rain, the finches with strong beaks have the most chance of survival. They can crack open old, tough seeds from the previous year. Birds with small beaks can't manage that. They die out. And the finches develop stronger and stronger beaks. Evolution in action!

I was SO exhausted on the journey back to the campsite, and to top it off, I had to carry that cool box with dead animals again. When we were on the coach, we had to report back on our discoveries, like real spies. (How life had begun. What skin colour Adam and Eve had. And which animal species had been found in which geological layers.) I told them all about Darwin and the finches' beaks. By the time I'd finished, half the class was ASLEEP.

"Don't take it personally," Mr Nolan said. "I thought it was extremely interesting."

"Me too!" said Christy. She stretched herself and yawned.

THE BEGINNING OF LIFE

How did life begin? No one really knows.

And when? Again, we don't know exactly.

But, thanks to fossils, scientists have discovered that 3.8 billion years ago there was already life on Earth.

THREE POINT EIGHT BILLION years ago. That's mind blowing!

But it's actually quite soon after the Earth came into being, if you remember that the Earth started out as a lump of waste in space with massive meteorites crashing into it...

But these meteorites weren't just destructive intruders. They also brought useful matter to the Earth, such as small molecules.

In space lots of different molecules float about. Molecules that are the building blocks for DNA, for example, and other molecules that make up your body. These molecules landed on Earth from space.

Under the right circumstances, these molecules can, like Lego bricks, click together and form bigger building blocks: this way, the first large molecules were formed. And when those molecules clump together into a small ball of fat, you may end up with something that almost looks like a very simple cell. Scientists don't know for sure, but this is probably how it happened: more and more molecules ended up in those balls – until, eventually, one became a real, living cell.

A single-cell organism like this wouldn't have been able to do very much. But at least it was alive!

4.54 BILLION YEARS IN 24 HOURS

We estimate that the Earth is 4.54 billion years old. Let's try and cram those 4.54 billion years into 24 hours. What would the day look like?

The clock starts ticking at midnight. Don't worry, you can stay in bed and carry on sleeping, as there's no life whatsoever in the first four hours.

It's not till four o'clock in the morning that you see the first signs of life – very simple single-cell animals.

During the daytime not much seems to be happening. If you were making this into a film, this part would be very boring. Only by 9 p.m. will you finally come across some animals with more than one cell.

At 11 p.m. the dinosaurs enter the scene.

And human beings? They only make an appearance in the last few seconds.

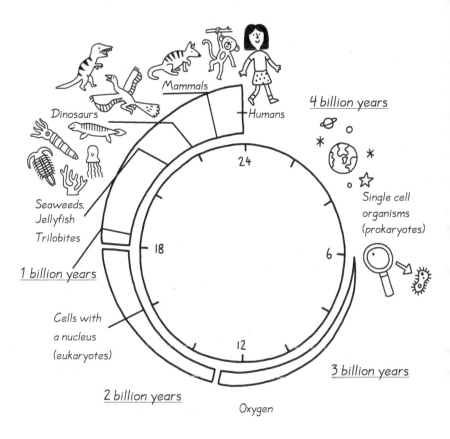

Mammals

Humans

Dinosaurs

4 billion years

24

Single cell
organisms
(prokaryotes)

Seaweeds,
Jellyfish
Trilobites

18

6

1 billion years

Cells with
a nucleus
(eukaryotes)

12

3 billion years

2 billion years

Oxygen

ALL THE PEOPLE!

*No one has ever kept track of exactly how many people have lived
on Earth.*

*But we can calculate how many ancestors you have. And how
many ancestors your friends have. In total there have probably
been some 100 billion people on Earth.*

There are currently about 7 billion people on Earth.

10,000 years ago there were only about 5 million people on Earth.

30,000 years ago there were probably only 20–30,000 people!

All people look very different from each other. Someone from Asia doesn't look like someone from Africa. A European doesn't resemble a Latin American. But mostly, we're almost exactly the same. In fact, if you look at our DNA, we are 99.9 per cent the same!

When we finally got back to the campsite, we weren't even allowed to have a rest, because Tony said that one of his chickens had been eaten and he knew for certain that it was those wolves. And he asked if we could please make sure we didn't leave anything, anything, ANYTHING lying around.

"Of course we won't leave anything lying around," said Mr Nolan. "By the way, do you happen to have a spade we could borrow?"

"I've got four," Tony said. "What is it for?"

"Nothing important," Mr Nolan said. "Just for fun."

Tony gave us four spades, and once he was out of sight, we quickly dug a hole. For the dead animals. It was a really tough job, because the soil was rock-hard and there were tree roots everywhere. But our hole was getting deeper and deeper.

"Hey, Sir," Matteo said suddenly. "I've got an idea! We can turn it into a trap, and we can put some pointy sticks at the bottom with the rabbits and rats stuck on. And the wolves will smell it and they'll come and fall into the trap, and then we can make a fire and we can roast them like a hog roast and eat them for dinner."

"That doesn't sound like a terribly good idea to me," Mr Nolan said.

"No," said Mehmet. "I'm not allowed pork. And neither are you, Rachid."

"Are you not allowed wolf meat either?" Matteo asked, surprised.

"You said pork!"

"No, I said wolf!"

Rachid frowned and looked at Mehmet. "Are we allowed wolf?"

Mehmet fished out his phone. "I'll text my mum to ask."

"We're not making a trap," Mr Nolan said firmly. "And we're not eating wolves, either. We'll bury the animals and cover the hole back up."

"But I can have the skins," Matteo said. "Because it was my idea."

"Matteo!" said Mr Nolan. "Are you listening to me?"

"I'll make a fur hat. With the tail still on."

THURSDAY NIGHT

"Sam!" Christy poked me. "We need your help. We have to come up with something for the talent show."

"I'll be there in a minute," I said.

"But you're on your phone!"

"Yeeeah. Just a minute!"

"Be a bit kinder to her!" said Florence. "You're going out together, remember?"

Sam:	Hey Uncle J
Sam:	we went to the Hancock museum
Sam:	it was awesome
Sam:	but I was thinking. Evolution and stuff. And the Big Bang.
Sam:	if you believe in those, can you still believe in God?

Jack:	Yes of course! Why not? I'm off to a birthday party, but I'll email you tonight, when I get back

"Hey Sam!" Archie entered the tent. "Are you coming? We've got a really cool idea for the talent show."

I put my phone under my pillow. "I'm not doing a sketch."

"No, of course not."

"And I'm not going to dance, either."

"Me neither."

"Or sing songs," I said. "Can't we do a scientific experiment? Like make a rocket with baking powder and vinegar?"

Archie shook his head. "No. We're going to perform surgery on Mr Nolan."

I stood up. Surgery on the teacher. That didn't sound too lame. "Come on. We're going to find Tony. We need to borrow a hand saw."

The talent show was much more fun than I had expected. Mehmet, Rachid, Luke, and Tom did a sketch about Little Red Riding Hood and the Big Bad Wolf. Luke was Little Red Riding Hood, with a little basket dangling from his arm, and for a skirt he had wrapped a towel around his waist, and when the wolf (Rachid) started to chase him, he ran off, but he tripped over his skirt which fell off and there he was, just with his boxers on. And the hunter (Tom) was laughing his head off so much he completely forgot that he had to catch the wolf, and then Rachid ate him up as well.

And then it was our turn, with Matteo, Christy, and Archie. "As you all know," Archie said, "Mr Nolan is often troubled by his appendix."

"Am I?" Mr Nolan said. "That's news to me!"

"Oh yes, Sir." Matteo ran to Mr Nolan, grabbed his hand and pulled him up. "Come with me, Mr Nolan. Please lie down on this table. We're going to do an operation."

"But I don't have any problems with my—"

"Oh yes you do," Archie said and he pushed Mr Nolan down by the shoulders. "It's been causing you a lot of grief."

Christy and I came on stage carrying a white sheet. We held it in front of the table, so nobody could see Mr Nolan. Archie switched on his torch. Now you could only see Mr Nolan's shadow. And Matteo's shadow, walking towards the table with a hand saw.

"NO!" shouted Mr Nolan. He waved his arms and legs around. "NO! PLEASE DON'T!"

Matteo peered at the audience from behind the sheet. He was holding a hammer in his hand. "First I'll need to anaesthetize him," he said, and he pretended to hit Mr Nolan on the head, and then he picked up the hand saw and started to saw open his stomach. He lifted all sorts of things out of Mr Nolan's stomach: a screwdriver and a pair of pincers and a hammer, and also the drilling machine we'd borrowed from Tony.

"Now, Sir," said Matteo. "Are you feeling better?"

"I'm feeling great!" said Mr Nolan. He stood up and stretched. "I fancy some toasted marshmallows. I bet it's time for our campfire."

"No!" Florence shouted. "We're doing a dance first."

"There's no need," said Archie.

But the music came on. Florence and Anna and Esther did this dance and they pretended to sing along. It was really lame, especially at the end, because they wanted us all to dance along with them. So we ran off and hid until the song was finished. It was past eleven o'clock when we went to bed. I secretly glanced at my phone to see if I had any emails.

From: Lydia Billington
To: Sam
Subject: Hi

Hi Sam

Everything OK? We miss you, darling. Please remember to change your boxers and socks every day. And don't forget to take a shower every day.

Love,
Mum xx

A shower every day? Haha. I'm not a girl. And clean socks every day? I didn't even know I had clean socks with me! I clicked away the email. And then I heard a ping. There was an email from Uncle Jack.

From: Professor Jack Scott McNeil
To: Sam Billington
Subject: Believing in God

Hey Sam,

I believe very strongly that you can believe in God AND take science seriously. The more I learn about evolution and the universe, the more I am in awe of God.

Not long ago I visited the European Southern Observatory again, an observatory based in South America, and there, miles away from the lights of the big cities, I saw the most impressive night sky. When I look at the stars, I am always deeply moved. Even when I was as young as you are now, when I visited the Outer Hebrides with your granny and grandpa and I stared at the millions of stars against the pitch-black night skies, I thought, "the universe is SO big and beautiful". God must be even bigger and more beautiful, as he's made all of this and he holds the enormous cosmos in his hands.

A lot of people have been touched like this. It inspired King David of the Bible to write a song 3,000 years ago (you can find it in the Bible: Psalm 19, verses 1–4):

The heavens tell all people about God's power.
The never-ending skies show everyone what God has made:
The sun, the moon and the stars.

Every day, heaven tells the story,
every night, heaven speaks,
with its own unique voice.

I think David expressed this in a wonderful way. I feel exactly the same about it. Because I went to university, I now know much more about the laws of nature and the processes that make it possible for stars to be formed. But all of this doesn't make any difference to my faith in the God of the Bible.

Every day I think: such greatness, what a breathtaking world we live in, what an amazing God we have.

Cheers,
Uncle Jack

I put my phone under my pillow.

FRIDAY

Our last day. I woke up smelling something unusual. It wasn't the smell of trees or sweaty socks. No, it was sweet and warm and like doughnuts. I climbed down from the top bunk and put my slippers on. Archie was still asleep. But Mr Nolan was outside, wearing an apron and juggling two enormous frying pans.

"Hey, Sam!" he said. "Good morning. You're up early. Would you like some French toast?"

"Some what? I asked.

Mr Nolan dropped another lump of butter into the frying pan. "French toast. Eggy bread."

The butter hissed in the pan, and it smelled so delicious, I'd said "yes please" before I knew it.

Mr Nolan gave me a plate with two slices of fried eggy bread, which had a thick layer of Nutella on. I'd never had such a delicious breakfast in my life.

"How do you make it, Sir?"

Mr Nolan fished four slices of white bread out of a bowl of milk, still dripping, and slid them into the frying pan. "It's easy: just whisk some milk and eggs together, add a bit of cinnamon, dip the bread in and fry it."

"This is scrumptious," I said with my mouth full.

"The bread was a bit stale," Mr Nolan explained. "I was worried you'd break your teeth on it, and then your mums would complain. So that's why I made it into eggy bread."

Christy and Anna emerged in their pjs, and Archie, Rachid, Tom, Luke, and Mehmet followed.

"What's that delicious smell?"

"Pancakes!"

"I am hungry!"

"Can I have one, Sir?"

"Woohoo. This is the best breakfast ever!"

"How do you make them, Sir? They look like slices of bread but they taste of doughnut!"

"It smells nice here," a familiar voice said. "Is there any left for me?"

Out from among the trees Reverend Richard appeared, walking towards us.

"Dad!" said Christy. "What are YOU doing here?"

"Great!" Mr Nolan said. "Our guest has arrived. Would you like some French toast, Reverend?"

"I'll have two, please," said Rev Rich. "And do you happen to have any coffee?"

The eggy bread was finished and we were all sitting around the large picnic table in the sunshine.

"How's the camp been so far?" Rev Rich asked.

"It's been epic," I said.

"Totally epic," said Christy.

"I prefer Thorpe Park," Tom said.

"And we learned a lot about evolution," said Archie. "And about the universe and stuff."

Rev Rich took a sip of his coffee. "And? What do you think? Now that you've done your own research?"

Archie hesitated. "I think that perhaps it's true after all. Evolution, I mean."

"No way!" said Anna. She shook her head and her ponytail swung from side to side. "Archie may think that, but I don't."

"Well, I do," said Christy.

"And so do I," I said.

"But..." Christy began. She crossed her arms and stared. I knew what she was thinking. "Yes," I said. "If the theory of evolution is true, is the Bible still true as well?"

"You see!" Anna called out. She banged her fist on the table. "Look what we've got ourselves into! Now you no longer believe in God!"

191

"We do!" I said crossly. "I DO believe in God!"

"And me too!" said Matteo, and he banged his fist so hard on the table that his glass fell over.

Orange juice spilt onto the floor.

"I have a suggestion," Rev Rich said. "Let's take a look at what the Bible says. Who has ever read the first few chapters of the Bible?"

"I know exactly what it says," said Anna.

"But have you ever carried on reading?" Rev Rich picked up his bag and took out a pile of sheets. "Here we go! Pass them round, please!"

We all got a printed handout of the first two chapters of the Bible.

SPOT THE DIFFERENCE

The creation story is told twice in the Bible. If you read it carefully, you will notice a few differences between the two accounts.

GENESIS 1

God made the heavens and the Earth
Day 1: God made light
Day 2: God made the sky
Day 3: God made the land, and plants, and trees, and sea
Day 4: God made the sun, moon, and stars
Day 5: God made the sea creatures and the birds
Day 6: God made the land animals and then human beings

GENESIS 2

One day, the Lord God made the heavens and the Earth. At the time nothing was growing on the Earth. There were no plants, because God hadn't sent rain yet. But there was water welling up from within the Earth. And the land was moist.

There were no people to work the land. Then the Lord God made man. He made him out of the dust. He breathed into his nostrils and the man came to life.

The Lord God made a garden in the east, in the land of Eden. He brought the man he had made into that garden. He made lots of different trees grow. The man was given the task of looking after the garden and cultivating it.

Then the Lord God thought: It isn't right for man to be alone. I'll make someone who can be a companion for him.

Then he made all the animals, wild and tame, and all the birds. He made them out of the dust.

Then the Lord God made the man fall into a deep sleep. And while the man was sleeping, God removed one of his ribs. The Lord God then used the rib to make a woman.

What is different about Genesis 2?

1. ....

2. ....

3. ....

4. ....

"Huh?" I scratched my forehead and read the bit again. "Did God make the plants first or the people first?"

"Plants!" shouted Anna.

"No! Look! First God made man!"

Christy poked me. "Do you see? Here it doesn't mention the six days at all!"

HOW DOES IT WORK?

If those two stories appeared in the newspaper, people would say: "Hey, this doesn't add up! On page one I read that God first made plants, animals next, and only then did he make people. But on page two it says: God first made man, then he created a garden with trees and plants, next he made animals, and only THEN did he make a woman."

People would send angry letters to the paper:
- *Your reporter must have been half asleep when he wrote this!*
- *These accounts can't both be true!*
- *So what was made first?!*

"Is it a fairytale?" Anna said crossly. "Is that what you're suggesting? That the Bible is a fairytale?"

Christy's dad shook his head. "No. That's not what I'm saying at all. But what we've just read isn't a report to be published in a newspaper, or in a scientific journal. The Bible isn't a manual for people in the twenty-first century, about exactly how the Big Bang or evolution happened. It's a very simple explanation of how God made everything. Personally I find the creation story very special. When you read it, you can just sense how much God loves people. How important he thinks they are. Isn't it special that the God who made the universe with such purpose and beauty wants to be in touch with us?"

HOW DO YOU EXPLAIN TO A TODDLER HOW A MOBILE PHONE WORKS?

- *Explain about radio waves, satellites, and radio masts, and exactly how they work*
- *Say: "Look, you can use this to talk to Mummy and Daddy. If*

you press this button, you can talk to them and hear them.
Even if you can't see them."

Which would your little brother or sister understand best, do you think?

The Bible was written thousands of years ago, well before telescopes and microscopes were invented. Most people couldn't even read. How did God make everything? The Bible explains it in such a way that people who lived thousands of years ago could understand God and his creation better.

What can we learn from the creation story in the Bible?
- God made everything
- God made the world like a house for mankind to live in
- The sun, moon, and stars aren't gods but objects that God has made
- God values people, they are important to him and he wants to have contact with them.
- God looks after people

"So it IS possible," Archie said. "You CAN believe in God and evolution."

"I think that is perfectly possible," Rev Rich said, nodding.

Mr Nolan wiped his forehead. "Phew. What a relief."

"We have tons of chocolate-chip cookies left," said Florence's mum, Karen. "And pink iced buns! Anyone for another drink?"

"A choc-chip cookie, please," I said.

"I'd like an iced bun!" said Christy.

"Hey, there's Tony," said Matteo. "Hi Tony, would you like a choc-chip cookie or a pink iced bun?"

"Neither," said Tony. "I just came to tell you that you don't need to worry anymore about this pack of wolves. It turns out they've crossed the border into Scotland."

"Go on, have a cookie," Mr Nolan insisted.

"All right then," said Tony.

"But if evolution is true," Esther said, "then the Earth wasn't a good place at all."

Christy's dad took a bite out of his iced bun. "Not a good place?"

"God said it was good, didn't he, after he made everything, the sun and the animals and so on?" said Esther. "Well, those animals died. And so did the people. I wouldn't call that good."

Christy's dad put his bun on the table, took off his glasses and started wiping the lens clean with a corner of his shirt. "When is something good?" he asked. He held up his glasses and asked: "When would you call a pair of glasses a good pair of glasses, for instance?"

I thought for a moment. "If you can see properly," I said. "If you can see everything."

"But wait. My glasses are really old fashioned."

"Yes, Dad!" Christy said. "You look so uncool. And you have goggle eyes when you're wearing them."

Rev Rich put his glasses back on. It was true. He did have goggle eyes. He looked a bit like a big friendly frog. "But I CAN see everything clearly," he said. "So I think it's a good pair of glasses. It does exactly what it's meant to do. What about a racehorse? When would you call a racehorse good?"

"If he can run really fast," said Archie. "If he wins races."

"And what if he's not a very friendly horse?" asked the vicar.

"It doesn't matter, if he's a champion," said Archie.

"So he does what he's supposed to be doing. I think it's the same with creation. God made a world that was exactly right for humans. A world in which they could live. A world in which people could get to know him. Maybe it wasn't a perfect world. But it was a good world."

Anna said: "Well, I still don't believe it at all. I believe that animals didn't die, in the beginning, before the fall."

"So what did frogs eat then?" asked Archie.

"I have no idea!" replied Anna. "I wasn't there."

Matteo put up his hand. "Hey, Rev Rich. Did Adam have a belly button?"

I rested my chin on my hands, and I thought about the explosion that started everything off, six weeks ago. The supermegaultraloudbangbang boomthis-is-the-end-of-the-world kind of bang.

I remembered how Uncle Jack had come to school to talk about the Big Bang and the universe, and that some of the parents had been angry, and that Mr Nolan had said we were going to do our own, proper research, to find out how God made everything. We had discovered a few things, but there were actually a lot of new questions that had come up, too. Like how you should interpret the Bible, and whether Adam had a mum and dad, and what the garden God made looked like, and why God had called the Earth good, when there were earthquakes and floods...

The sun was rising above the pine trees and it tickled my neck.

I looked up. It was just as if I was looking at the sun for the very first time.

As if the sun was suddenly something truly special.

The sun actually was truly special. It was our own private star that brings warmth to the Earth, and light. Warmth and light that enable trees to grow, and plants and animals and people to thrive.

So far away. Yet exactly near enough.

So big. But so small compared to the other stars.

Then I stopped thinking about all those questions. I thought about the tiny speck of dust that was too heavy to be lifted. Perhaps God was holding it in his hand, nearly 14 billion years ago. And then he blew on it as if it was dandelion fluff and said: "Let there be light."

God was there before the sun. God was there before the Big Bang.

Fourteen billion years ago.

Did God really have to wait so long before we arrived on the scene? Wasn't that boring?

But perhaps he was already thrilled with the first amoeba. With the dinosaurs and the jellyfish. With the trilobites and the lungfish. And with the first flying dinosaur.

Perhaps for God it didn't matter how long it all took.

Just thinking about all this made me feel slightly dizzy.

Bigger than the sun. Bigger than our universe and all the other universes put together. Bigger than everything.

And still so very close.

So close that he could hear me.

"Hello, God," I whispered. "I love the way you made everything in this world. It's totally awesome."

ABOUT THE AUTHORS

Corien exploring the Naturalis Biodiversity Center in Leiden, researching for the book

Corien Oranje is a Dutch children's author, journalist, and theologian. In the Netherlands she is best known for her books *Champion; Love You, Miss You;* and *Don't Eat the Teacher*. With her books *Storm in the Bath* and *Tropical Conspiracy* she has twice won a prize for Christian children's literature. Corien is often invited into schools to talk about her books or to lead writing workshops. As a journalist, she particularly enjoys interviewing interesting people.

Corien is married to Dick and together they have four sons (including triplets). They lived in Indonesia for a decade, but have since moved back to the Netherlands. Corien belongs to a Protestant church in the north of the Netherlands (Groningen) where her husband is the vicar and two of their sons play guitar in the music group.

Corien is an excellent swimmer, at least for her age (fifty-three). But if you asked her what she isn't good at, she'd say running and playing the violin. If you want to find out more about Corien, visit:

www.corienoranje.nl (in Dutch).

Cees Dekker is a Dutch professor at the Delft University of Technology. Many years ago he studied physics, and a bit of astronomy too, but his current research is primarily in nanotechnology and cell biology. He experiments with DNA molecules to find out how 2 metres of DNA fit into each of our cells, where it is rolled into a small ball of only 0.002 millimetres wide. He also researches how bacteria split. And he's been trying to build cells by creating small soap bubbles that replicate this splitting process.

Cees in his university lab

Cees Dekker is married with three children. He is a Christian and an active member of an evangelical church in the west of the Netherlands, where he regularly leads services or plays the guitar. He has written some books about faith and science; for example, *Learned and Faithful*.

If you want to find out more about Cees, visit:
www.ceesdekkerlab.tudelft.nl

WHY DID THEY WRITE THIS BOOK?

Corien Oranje: I was pretty bad at physics and failed my final physics school exams. My father thought this was a great shame (he is a physicist), but it was just the way it was.

However, I was very good at making up stories. And I could say, "Hello, how are you?" in seven different languages. At the same time, I couldn't work out the physical force of a kilo of air onto a kilo of water, or the speed at which a brick falls from a tower. I had absolutely no idea. And, in fact, I wasn't interested either. I'd rather write books, I thought. Who would have known that one day I was going to write a book with a university professor who knows ALL about physics and biology and about tiny, tiny cells, and about how life began?

For the first time in my life I discovered that physics can be fun and gravity can be cool! I have also found out that zooming into a tiny blood cell is just as extraordinary as floating in space, in between the stars.

To be honest, I never really knew what to think about the Big Bang and the theory of evolution. I remember my indignation when my Year Six teacher suggested that God had perhaps created the world through an evolutionary process. That couldn't be right, I thought. Surely that's not what it says in the Bible? God made heaven and earth in six days. It's as simple as that. After secondary school, I went on to study theology. I learnt about God and the Bible, about God's salvation plan and the new world Jesus talks about. I carefully examined Bible verses and dug deep to find their meaning. And I enjoyed showing children and young people how awesome the Bible is!

But I quickly learned that not all young people think the Bible is awesome. They often struggle with their faith. At their Christian schools they had been taught, just like me, that God made everything in six days. But at university they learned about the Big Bang and evolution. So what should they believe?

One day I interviewed Cees Dekker, a super-intelligent professor who has won lots of prizes and has made some amazing discoveries. Despite all his achievements, he was really humble and down to earth. He was also full of enthusiasm when he told me how God made the universe, the world, and people so beautifully. Professor Cees Dekker taught me that we don't have to be afraid of science. We can freely explore the natural world and space, as this is how we find out how God made everything. And if you carefully investigate, measure, and calculate, you will find out that there was a Big Bang about 14 billion years ago. And that life evolved over a period of billions of years.

I thought this was awesome, and that children should find out about it, too, before they leave secondary school, and go to college or university. I wanted to reassure them that there is actually nothing to worry about. As a Christian you don't need to be afraid of what's been discovered about the Big Bang and evolution. I even dreamed about this one night! When I woke up, I tweeted, "Last night I dreamed that I was writing a book with Cees Dekker about the Big Bang, the Bible, and this creation business!" In less than five minutes Cees replied, "Brilliant idea!"

So we decided to write a book together. It was amazing

to discover so much about the universe and about how life began. Physics is much more fun than I used to think. And the more I learned, the more I discovered that God is much more powerful and fabulous than I had ever imagined.

Cees Dekker: I've been thinking about how God created the world for a very long time. I've read hundreds of books and have had thousands of conversations. And in the end, I came to this simple conclusion: God created the world through a long evolutionary process. This is how God made the world, including people, who hold a very special place in his heart.

When I was at primary school, I didn't worry much about these things. We knew from the Bible that God had created the world. And if science discovered that this had happened through an evolutionary process, then apparently that was the way he had done it. No problem whatsoever.

Much later though, by the time I was already a professor, I started to think about it again. Some scientists were saying that you really can't believe in God if you properly understand the theory of evolution. They said that evolution and faith in God are incompatible. For years I felt challenged when working out how evolution and the Bible could be compatible, and what exactly we can learn from the Bible and from science. I soon discovered that it's ludicrous to say that you can't believe in God if the world came into being by evolution. Science, including evolutionary science, is about lots of interesting, measurable "knowledge facts" about the world – the origin of stars, how DNA works, how new species of animals are formed... But it isn't about God. Science simply doesn't say anything about God.

We can learn about God through the Bible. At the heart of it is Jesus, who did and taught incredible things. But of course, the Bible starts with the famous creation stories. Here we read about the God who made the world. I have learned a lot about these creation stories from Bible scholars, professors who know a lot about the Biblical text and about the ancient Near-Eastern culture of that time. These stories are not about evolution, DNA, or strata with fossils. Instead they tell us about the Almighty God of love who is creator of all that exists, who loves people, and who wants to relate to them and care for them.

I am really glad I can have the assurance that God is there. That the universe is not a mere coincidence without any purpose. For me it has become increasingly clear that science and the Christian faith are actually wonderfully compatible.

Quite often, I run into people who tell a very different story. Who no longer believe in God because "it doesn't make sense". Who, as children, heard the creation story at home, and later on, when they went to university, learned that the world came into being through an evolutionary process. And who then concluded that the one story is true, and the other isn't, and then stopped believing in God. What a shame! It doesn't have to be this way.

Many times I've thought: how great would it be if children and teenagers heard much earlier that it is definitely possible to believe in God and at the same time have fun exploring how everything works in the world, learning about the Big Bang and the evolution of life into everything we see around us now. I concluded that one day, someone should write a book about this.

And then, three years ago, I met Corien Oranje. She

came to interview me for a Dutch magazine. I thought she was a fabulous and funny person. She's someone who can talk even faster than me (and that means really fast). Someone with a great sense of humour. And someone who writes the most amazing children's books. So we got together and decided to jointly write a children's book. And this is the result!

Personally I think it's become a pretty cool book. It's really funny, has a great storyline, and readers learn lots of interesting facts along the way. But I especially like the fact that Sam, his teacher, and his friends are such an inquisitive bunch, always eager to explore and learn. Remember when the teacher, Mr Nolan, says to his class, "We're at school to learn, right? So let's do our own research. Let's go and find out for ourselves." That's how it should be!

And you see that same openness in Christy's dad, Rev Rich, the local vicar. He helps them to investigate what the Bible actually says about creation, and to understand the meaning and purpose of the first chapters of the Bible.

I hope that you really enjoyed this book. And that you have learned that it is definitely possible to wholeheartedly believe in God, even if you know everything there is to know about fossils, dinosaurs, stars, and more! Because he is the One who made it all.